T0001453

# MULTIPLYING DISCIPLES

# MULTIPLYING DISCIPLES

A toolkit for learning to live like Jesus

Phil Wilthew

malcolm down
PUBLISHING

Copyright © 2018 Phil Wilthew

First published in 2018 by Malcolm Down Publishing Ltd
www.malcolmdown.co.uk

The right of Phil Wilthew to be identified as the author of this work has
been asserted by him in accordance with the Copyright, Designs and
Patents Act 1988.

All rights reserved. No part of this publication may be reproduced, stored
in a retrieval system, or transmitted in any other form or by any means,
electronic, mechanical, photocopying, recording or otherwise, without the
prior permission of the publisher.

**British Library Cataloguing in Publication Data**
A catalogue record for this book is available from the British Library.

ISBN 978-1-910786-87-1

Unless otherwise indicated, Scripture quotations are taken from The Holy
Bible, New International Version (Anglicised edition), copyright ©1979,
1984, 2011 by Biblica (formerly International Bible Society). Used by
permission of Hodder & Stoughton Publishers, an Hachette UK company.
All rights reserved.

Scripture quotations marked NLT are taken from The Holy Bible, New Living
Translation, copyright © 1996, 2004, 2015 by Tyndale House Foundation.
Used by permission of Tyndale House Publishers, Inc., Carol Stream, Illinois
60188, USA. All rights reserved.

Scripture quotations marked ESV are taken from The Holy Bible, English
Standard Version, copyright © 2001 by Crossway Bibles, a division of Good
News Publishers.

Cover design by Toby Cosh

Printed and bound by CPI Group (UK) Ltd, Croydon, CR0 4YY

# What Others Are Saying...

'As I have spent some time with the leaders of Catalyst over the last few years, I have been deeply impressed with their passion for Jesus, their commitment to following the way of mission and discipleship, and their resolve to multiply out what God is doing in their midst. In this book, Phil Wilthew takes us on a journey through the things they have learned, the tools they have developed and many of their stories of encounter with God and breakthrough of his kingdom. If you are looking for an authentic walk with Jesus where you can grow in spiritual passion, community and mission, then I would strongly recommend that you read this book.'

*Paul Maconochie, 3DM Team Leader for USA and Canada, 3DMovements.com*

'I am more and more convinced that the greatest challenge for local churches today is effective discipleship. It's brilliant that Phil Wilthew has created this brilliant, practical equipping tool, distilled from many years as a skilled practitioner, serving churches and making disciples of Jesus Christ.'

*Pete Greig, 24-7 Prayer International and Emmaus Rd Guildford*

'Phil is an amazing pastor, mentor, pioneer and coach and I would recommend no one better to bring fresh revelation on the topic of discipleship! We need this badly in the body of Christ!'

*Sean Feucht, founder of the global worship and missions movement Burn 24/7; author and worship leader with Bethel Music Collective*

'I have found what Phil shares in this book to be hugely helpful in discipling the congregations I lead in London. I'd recommend it to anybody who is looking for some simple, helpful tools for making strong disciples of Jesus today.'

*Phil Moore, leader of Everyday Church London and author of the* Straight to the Heart *series of commentaries*

'Phil Wilthew's excellent book *Multiplying Disciples* presents a necessary antidote to consumerist Christianity and failure to grow into maturity. It demonstrates how grace-filled, Spirit-empowered disciple-making is the responsibility of each local church. I commend it to you.'

*David Devenish, international apostolic leader within Newfrontiers movement of churches, speaker and author of* Fathering Leaders, Motivating Mission: Restoring the Role of the Apostle in Today's Church

'I have used many of these tools on multiple occasions with lots of different people. What I love is seeing the light bulb go on in people's minds as they get greater revelation of who God is, who they are, and how they can have the influence God has called them to have on the earth. Churches are not meant to be filled with consumers; rather we have the responsibility to train, equip and empower our people to follow Jesus really closely and reveal him wherever they have influence. These tools, and Phil's introductions to them, will inspire those who access them to fall more in love with Jesus as they go on a journey to increasingly understand what it means to be his disciple.'

*Wendy Mann, author of* Naturally Supernatural *and international speaker*

# Acknowledgements

Discipleship is a team sport and this book on discipleship is no different. A number of years ago, in a desire to keep building a growing and mission-minded church, a small team of colleagues from The King's Arms Church, Bedford, UK began to explore the secrets behind one of the most rapidly growing churches in the UK at the time. As we visited this thriving community we found the answer but it was perhaps not the one we were expecting. Discipleship. Missional fruit is the tip of the iceberg. The real key is what happens under the surface. If you create real disciples, mission will happen naturally.

This one meeting kick-started a chain of events, one of which is the publication of this book and the attempt, in our own home church, to put these things into practice. While I have authored the words on these pages, the design, concept, heart and energy has come from more than me alone. Special thanks go to Karen Buttery, Steve Wilson and Simon Holley, the original group-life research team, who were the brains and the brilliance behind so much of what this book contains. Look what we created! Working with you on this project has been such a thrill and honour. Thank you for all your efforts and input. This is your book as much as anyone's.

Jane Sanders has been a phenomenal gift from God in the editing process and has given many hours in helping iron out my bad grammar and make this book much more readable. Thank you, Jane, for your eye for detail and general encouragement along the way. I am so grateful for you. Thanks also go to Toby Cosh and Steve Wilson for hours spent on designing front covers and graphics. Legends one and all.

On a personal level I look back at the small but significant number of people who have invested in my own life as a disciple of Jesus. I have learnt how to follow Christ through the example and wisdom of some real-life heroes, who, through laying their lives down have taught me what real leadership love looks like.

Huge gratitude goes to my parents who have consistently demonstrated Christ to me, whether through the night-time patience of my childhood eczema-induced sleeplessness or the generosity of helping us buy our first home. The youth leaders who opened their homes and families to me left a mark, which will never be forgotten. Ian Chalmers, Bob Hollway and Jon Ridgwell – you will never know how grateful I am for the kindness and faithfulness shown to teenage Phil, with all of his immaturity, insecurities and need for great role models. Thank you for the search for the best chips in Brighton. Thank you for the tiramisu. Thank you for all the mess you cleared up after me. Thank you for your spiritual fathering. Thank you.

I am also discipled daily by my own family. Carole, you model passion for God, perseverance in prayer, sacrificial love and compassion for the broken. Most of my best stories involve you because you are the heart of this home. Lauren, you light up my world with your creativity, love for people, generosity of spirit and heart for justice. You are God's beautiful gift to me and I learn from you constantly. Sam, your diligence, passion for excellence, single-minded focus and gentlemanly conduct make me so proud. God said you would delight our hearts and you do.

Lastly, a huge thank you and acknowledgement goes to Mike Breen (michaeljamesbreen.com) and 3DM (3dmovements.com), the inspiration behind the creation of a discipleship language in the first place. Thank you for your visionary gift and the provocation to create naturally multiplying discipleship cultures. We particularly recognise Mike's inspiration with our PLAY tool, which he has so helpfully written and taught on. We would strongly recommend readers of this book to also purchase Mike's book *Building a Discipling Culture: How to release a missional movement of discipling people like Jesus did* (3DM Publishing, 2017).

I hope as you read the pages of this book you receive tools that equip you to do the work of the kingdom where God has placed you. Go and make disciples of all nations. Make Jesus famous.

Phil Wilthew

# Dedications

This book is dedicated to my children, Lauren and Sam, the two people it has been my greatest joy to play a part in discipling. Run hard after Jesus. Fix your eyes on him. What you have freely received, go and give away. You both rock my world.

Hold on to the pattern of wholesome teaching you learned from me – a pattern shaped by the faith and love that you have in Christ Jesus. Through the power of the Holy Spirit who lives within us, carefully guard the precious truth that has been entrusted to you. (2 Timothy 1:13–14 NLT)

# Contents

# Foreword by Simon Holley

And Jesus came and said to them, 'All authority in heaven and
on earth has been given to me. Go therefore and make disciples
of all nations, baptising them in the name of the Father and of
the Son and of the Holy Spirit, teaching them to observe all that I
have commanded you. And behold, I am with you always, to the
end of the age.' (Matthew 28:18–20 ESV)

Neil Cole, author of *Organic Church*, writes: 'Ultimately, each church
will be evaluated by only one thing – its disciples. Your church is only
as good as her disciples. It does not matter how good your praise,
preaching, programmes or property are; if your disciples are passive,
needy, consumeristic, and not [radically obedient] your church is not
good.'[i]

It's a sobering quote for those of us who are leaders of churches and
it never ceases to elicit a groan when I read it aloud. The truth of
it is self-evident and painful and there's no doubt about it; building
churches that make naturally multiplying disciples is a critical need in
the Western church today.

One time I stood talking to a friend, a busy pastor like myself, about
how he lived out the command of Jesus to 'go and make disciples'.
When he had finished talking I couldn't help but blurt out, 'But, Paul,
how do you fit it all in?' Without a pause, he turned and looked me
squarely in the eyes. 'That question is your problem, Simon. Fit it
in? Isn't it what Jesus commanded us to do? To make disciples was
his last and final command. Our question should not be how we fit
discipleship in. Instead we should do what Jesus told us to do first and
then worry about how we fit everything else in.'

Ouch. They tell us that 'faithful are the wounds of a friend'; but why does faithful have to leave a stinging red mark?

There have been a number of turning points in my life and this moment definitely counts as one of them. I suddenly realised that a number of my excuses, busyness being probably the top one, were simply that. Excuses. That one day I would have to give an account for my life and I was being given the opportunity for a mid-race course correction. I was determined to take it. But not only me. I was going to take as many people with me as I could!

That short conversation perhaps illustrates the issue that many of us have when it comes to this issue of making disciples. We want to do what Jesus told us to do. But the busyness of life pushes it down the priority list. Or perhaps it's the fact that we haven't been properly discipled ourselves; how can I give away what I've never received, we cry? Or perhaps it's that we don't feel that we know enough, or are mature enough, or are 'ready'. That all encompassing spiritual sounding reason that is hard to argue with but impossible to define.

What would it look like, though, to see these excuses as they really are? To expose them in the light of Jesus' command to make disciples and refuse to hide any longer from his words. What would it look like to focus the energy of our churches not simply on more programmes and meetings but instead to shape a community around a single desire; to build the type of church that repeatedly makes the types of disciples who go on to change the world, naturally reproducing as they do. To shape a people who have an intentionality about disciple-making that keeps them focused on the task in hand, seeking the Lord's help where they become stuck or not able to move forward.

That's what we set out to do. Not just in one church but in every church that we are connected to. We went back to basics on the whole theme of discipleship and started with a blank piece of paper. We reread the

Bible through a new lens. We studied the methods of the early church and other more recent writers. There were a number of key things we learned during that period, but none more important than the reality that for disciples to multiply they have to not only model a life worth multiplying but also be able to teach others how to give it away to others. Those groups that were multiplying had simple concepts that were easy to teach and pass on to others. Yet when asked even the simplest of questions, many of our people would point others to 'read this book', or 'watch this video' or 'I'll send you a link to a PowerPoint later'. This reliance on second-hand information meant that key information was often never read, watched or flicked through and the discipleship process broke down. The ability to simply communicate timeless biblical truths in a way that others could also repeat had largely been lost.

That's when we discovered 'Lifeshapes' pioneered by Mike Breen and others who are part of the 3DM movement. Their example inspired us to create our own discipleship toolkit that fit in our context and enabled us to begin to raise up those who could equip others. Having a consistent language is certainly not the only thing critical to creating a movement of multiplying disciples, but it certainly helps. It enables people to learn and then put into practice the critical principles that are important to the Christian life. It enables them also to teach others to do the same. This toolkit is the foundation that we use to raise up the types of people that we believe ultimately go on to change the world. It's designed to be simple and memorable and all encompassing enough to give people a solid foundation in living the Christian life. It's aimed at anyone who wants to take a deeper journey to become more like Jesus and in the process gain the tools to help others do the same.

When we thought about who from our team would be best to condense our learning into book form, Phil Wilthew was the first name to come to mind. I have worked with Phil now for over seven years and his grasp of scripture, creative ability to communicate timeless truths and understanding of the key issues involved in raising world-changers is second to none. I can't recommend this book enough. I believe it carries a timely message for the church today.

**Notes**

i. Neil Cole, *Organic Church: Growing Faith Where Life Happens* (Jossey Bass, 2005).

# About The King's Arms and This Book

The King's Arms is a Christian church, started in 1992, that has grown to be a community of over 1,000 people from all different ages, stages and walks of life. Our purpose is to live life the way Jesus said that it should be: caring for each other, enjoying diversity and creativity, reaching out to those around us and living with honesty and authenticity.

This book is the culmination of years of study, as we've sought to provide the church with a language around which we can *learn to live like Jesus.* It is very much a work in progress and we are still on a journey learning to use these materials in a healthy and fruitful way. I doubt that this journey will ever cease this side of eternity!

To get the best out of *Multiplying Disciples: Learning to Live Like Jesus,* it is vital to approach it as much as a toolbox as a piece of literature. Much of my own toolbox at home was handed down to me by my grandfather, who was a keen craftsman and general fix-it kind of man. Drills, spanners and screwdrivers all came from him and I have laboured to learn how to use them through the years, with varying degrees of success! When it comes to discipleship, it is also critical that we have a toolbox to turn to in the development of men and women who run after Jesus.

Disciple is a word that simply means 'learner'. Good tools enable us to learn to live the Jesus way effectively because they are easily reproducible, explainable and memorable. My grandfather's tools have been effective through several generations because they were designed to be simple enough to be used again and again.

Good tools also help us to multiply beyond ourselves. Jesus' call is to make disciples in all nations. This requires a shift in our mindsets to one of replication and empowerment. We are all called to make disciples who, in turn, make disciples. Having a toolbox of discipleship enables this to happen much more effectively because it gives us a common place to start and a common language to speak. It means that we can all play our part, young or old, new believer or well established. We are all called to make disciples of Jesus.

In this book, these tools are all framed around the three dimensions of our connection with God (UP), our growing character in community (IN) and walking in our calling to change the world (OUT). The healthy disciple has these three dimensions to their lives.

In each of these three parts of the book a selection of tools is given for use in our own lives and those that we are helping to grow in God. The tools selected are certainly not exhaustive and there will be many others in the arsenal of the disciple-maker that I have not had time or space to detail. However, there is method in the madness! Great attention has been given to try and reflect the tools that, as a team, we felt were essential and effective in bringing growth and maturity to people. These are not cerebral tools produced without reference to real life. These are tools that have proven to bring forth fruit and breakthrough in the lives of individuals and, in some cases, whole teams. They are certainly a great starting place for raising the kind of disciples who believe they are born to change the world.

After each tool is outlined, a brief section called 'View from the Front Line' will appear, that aims to put some light and colour into what has just been read, in the form of real-life stories and expanded thoughts. Tools, read on their own, can be pretty cold. My hope is that as you read the tool and View from the Front Line together, it will form a compelling picture of what discipleship looks like in that particular area.

The additional use of symbols is also very deliberate because so many of us are visual learners with brains that often remember shapes and patterns more than words. All of our tools are based around common audio or computer symbols that appear on most desktops around the world and form something of a universal language for most people. We have depicted these symbols deliberately simply because we want them to be easily replicated wherever we might find ourselves discipling others. Whether that be around the family dining table or in the local coffee shop, these tools are simple enough to be sketched on the back of an envelope, because so often the best discipleship happens in the course of everyday life.

# Introduction: The Future Belongs to Learners

'If my life is fruitless, it doesn't matter who praises me, and if my life is fruitful, it doesn't matter who criticises me.' So said John Bunyan, the most famous son of Bedford, the English market town in which this book is now being written. In 1678, John Bunyan published *The Pilgrim's Progress,* his allegorical tale of Christian, a spiritual adventurer who, through many tests and trials, eventually reaches the Celestial City of God. One of the most famous works in English literature, it was largely written during the twelve years Bunyan spent in Bedford jail, where he was imprisoned for holding non-conformist Christian gatherings, an illegal activity at the time. His story paints a vivid picture of a Christian who was learning to live life and bear fruit the Jesus way: *The Pilgrim's Progress* is ultimately about discipleship.

In the church that I am part of, The King's Arms (yes, I know it sounds like an English public house), we have been on a journey of rediscovering what it looks like to be a disciple of Jesus. As *The Pilgrim's Progress* teaches us, maturity in Christ is not just about crossing a finishing line, but running a race, a long race, a marathon that includes steep gradients, bends in the road, unexpected detours and moments of surprise, mystery and wonder. Being a disciple of Jesus is an ongoing process, not a one-off event; a relationship, not a ritual; a lifelong journey with Jesus, learning to live life his way and being transformed by walking close beside him on the road. Progress for the pilgrim looks like connection to the King and his kingdom: we believe it's time for another discipleship revolution.

## The Future Belongs to Learners

'Disciple', at its most basic level, means 'follower' or 'apprentice'. The Greek word used in the New Testament for disciple is *mathetes,* which simply means 'learner', occurring 262 times, thus underlining its centrality in the Christian life. Indeed, it would be difficult to over-estimate how much Jesus' first disciples must have learnt as they followed him from village to village, seeing the kingdom breaking out and lives being changed. Life must have been a continuous series of shocks to the spiritual solar-plexus as they re-learnt how to think, prioritise, pray, serve, love, forgive and relate the Jesus way. Later, those same disciples became leaders and disciple-makers themselves, but they never stopped being learners. The point at which any of us choose to stop learning is the point at which we stop growing, stop being effective and begin to find ourselves at a distance from Jesus and his kingdom purposes. Lifelong learners become life-changing leaders. The future of the world belongs to learners.

Jesus' ultimate purpose is the same as it was in the beginning – to release men and women who bear the image of God to go into all the earth so that it will be filled with the knowledge of his glory. And his chosen method is discipleship – restoring us to our image-bearing nature, so that we can re-present the Father to a sin-diseased creation as we learn what it is like to live as sons and daughters of the King, caught up in his business – his family business – of bringing heaven to earth. While the cross put to death our old nature with all its sickness and proclivity to reject God, Jesus' resurrection has made us brand-new creations, born again into the Father's family and in the process of being transformed to think and behave like our saviour and elder brother Jesus.

Jesus' discipleship model has now become our mandate for multiplication, and the goal of this book is to help release radical disciple-making disciples all over the world, who can perpetuate the glory of God wherever they go, into every sphere of society. Dallas Willard says:

> The greatest issue facing the world today, with all its heartbreaking needs, is whether those who, by profession or culture, are identified as 'Christians' will become disciples – students, apprentices, practitioners – of Jesus Christ, steadily learning from him how to live the life of the Kingdom of the Heavens into every corner of human existence.[1]

This is indeed the greatest issue, particularly in the context of much popular Christian culture, which can misleadingly equate raising a hand in a church service to following Jesus. Clearly, the one can lead to the other, but not necessarily so. Making a one-time public response is a fantastic start but no more than that, in the same way that a wedding does not make a marriage but merely marks and celebrates its beginning. Christian discipleship is not a one-off event, but a radical, all-consuming, lifelong lifestyle of learning to run after Jesus in the upward, inward and outward dimensions of our lives. Eric Russ rightly points out the following:

> A Christian disciple is one who loves God with everything one has. A Christian disciple, by God's grace, becomes more and more like Christ through a life of faith and obedience.[2]

So what does it look like, this life of loving God with everything that one has?

### The Three Dimensions of Discipleship

> 'Come, follow me,' Jesus said, 'and I will send you out to fish for people.' At once they left their nets and followed him. (Matthew 4:19–20)

As Peter and Andrew put down their nets to follow Jesus, they little knew what a challenging, exhilarating and transformational new life it would be. It would shape them in the three dimensions of human existence; namely, our relationship with God, the growth of our own character in community, and our mission to serve others with the gospel.

We might imagine it like this: God the Father is the potter, we are the clay and Jesus is the model. The Father has his hands on our lives, shaping, moulding, changing, restoring and ultimately fashioning us to look like the model, his own dear Son, Jesus. By the power of the Spirit at work within us, the Father is forming us into the likeness of Christ. This is discipleship – the intentional process of allowing ourselves to be shaped by the goodness of God in his Trinitarian glory. The apostle Paul expresses the same Trinitarian concept, using architectural language, as he declares that we are simultaneously *God's* building, built on the foundation of *Christ* and are living temples of the *Spirit* (1 Corinthians 3:7–17). In other words, the three dimensions of discipleship are built upon the nature of God himself in all of his three-dimensional personhood. We are called to know the Father, create Christ-centred cultures and extend the kingdom in the power of the Spirit.

The very second Peter and Andrew stepped out of that fishing boat, the Father began to shape them to look like Jesus in the power of the Spirit, as he does with every one of us who follow him. You are called to be like God because you are made in his image.

Mike Breen helpfully labels these three dimensions UP, IN and OUT.[3] These are the three areas in which learning takes place for the disciple of Jesus and we will explore each of these three themes in more detail later in the book. For now, here is a quick summary of our three-dimensional learning.

## UP: Learning to Connect to God

*'Come and follow me.'* Our first calling is to know the Father as Jesus does. The first call of the disciple is to come to him. Disciples are those who actively grow their friendship with God through prayer, worship, the prophetic and studying the Scriptures.

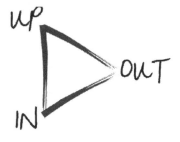

I believe there was something so utterly captivating, awesome and other worldly about Jesus that these tough, down-to-earth fishermen could not help but leave everything so they could follow him. They were willing to trade all their security, comfort, familiarity and family expectations, just so they could be with him.

## IN: Learning to develop our Character in Community

*'Come and follow me and I will make you . . .'* Secondly, disciples are those who are growing on the inside through connection on the outside! Jesus promises to make something of us; he comes to shape our ideas, our identity and, as a natural consequence, our behaviour and attitudes too, and the way that he does this is often through other people.

Peter and Andrew would find their mind-set continually challenged as they followed Jesus and caught his perspective on truth, priorities and meaning. Jesus has not come to be a subtle influence on the edge of our lives – one voice among many. He has come to take up management of our hearts, minds and emotions. Disciples partner with Jesus in learning how to think and live as he does and how to live in community as God intended us to. We change and learn through community and connection with others.

## OUT: Learning to fulfil our Calling

*'I will make you fishers of men.'* Thirdly, disciples have an outward mission for their lives and a sense of purpose in the world. We do not exist just for ourselves, but to serve others around us. Jesus helps us discover the gifts he has given us, teaches us how to bring the influence of his kingdom in the world and enables us to make more disciples for him.

As Jesus called Peter and Andrew, he promised to fashion them into world changers – 'I will teach you how to fish for people!' Jesus is equally committed today to catching us up in his amazing mission to win disciples from every tribe, nation and tongue (Revelation 5:9). Each one of us has a part to play in God's mission, whether it is at the school gate, in the lecture hall, at our work desks or in our communities and amongst our friends. George MacLeod, founder of the Iona Community and a minister of the Church of Scotland, summed up our mission well when he said:

> The cross must be raised again at the centre of the marketplace as well as on the steeple of the church. I am claiming that Jesus was not crucified in a cathedral between two candles, but on a cross between two thieves; on the town garbage heap, at a crossroads so cosmopolitan they had to write His title in Hebrew, Latin, and Greek. At the kind of place where cynics talk smut, and thieves curse, and soldiers gamble, because that is where he died and that is what he died about and that is where churchmen ought to be and what churchmen should be about.[4]

We want to raise up the kind of radical, multiplying, disciple-making disciples who actually believe they are called to change the world: men and women who are on the front foot in serving their communities, neighbourhoods, economies, cultures, schools and places of influence.

Ultimately, God is interested in raising up not only some big churches, but some big people. A church's true effectiveness is seen not in its seating capacity, but in its sending capacity. True disciples of Jesus are by nature missional, engaged and ready to play their part in the great commission.

## The Power of Influence; the Power of Proximity

This process of learning to love God with everything one has cannot happen in a vacuum. It happens in the context of community and friendship with other people: in other words, in the church. While many people have given up on the church, Jesus has not. Scripture is clear that God's purposes for the planet are still firmly wrapped up in it:

> His intent was that now, through the church, the manifold wisdom of God should be made known to the rulers and authorities in the heavenly realms, according to his eternal purpose that he accomplished in Christ Jesus our Lord. (Ephesians 3:10–11)

God has a high view of the church and has chosen it as the means through which he helps us grow as disciples of Jesus. We need each other! It is impossible to establish heaven's value system of forgiveness, sacrificial love, honour and generosity if we have no one that we need to forgive, love sacrificially, honour and express generosity towards. We were made to grow in a culture of connection and without it we cannot grow as God intends, because we need one another. The opportunity to live authentic and vulnerable lives with others is as fundamental to life as breathing and eating. 'Vulnerability is the birthplace of innovation, creativity and change,' says Brene Brown in her TED talk 'The Power of Vulnerability',[5] and that is true, because God designed us to help create change in one another in an atmosphere of trust, loyalty, honesty and love.

While programmes and methods have their usefulness, lasting change happens most readily in the context of relationships and community.

Leroy Eims, who served for over fifty years with the Navigators, an organisation dedicated to the art of making disciples, says the following:

> Why are fruitful, dedicated, mature disciples so rare? The biggest reason is that all too often we have relied on programmes or material or some other thing to do the job. The work of the ministry is to be carried on by people . . . ultimately people cannot be helped by some thing but must be helped by someone. Disciples *cannot* be mass produced. We cannot drop people into a 'programme' and see disciples emerge at the end of the production line. It takes time to make disciples.[6]

We do not become disciples only by attending a meeting or a training course. While these can help, we actually need people who can look into the whites of our eyes, accept us, know us, love us and call the best out of us. Lasting influence flows from real relationships.

Sociologists estimate that even the most introverted individual will influence at least 10,000 people in their lifetime. Whether or not you consider yourself a leader, you are significant. Discipleship is the art of Christ-centred influence. The real question a disciple of Jesus must answer is not, 'Will I have influence in my lifetime?' but, 'What will I do with the influence I have? Whose life am I called to influence for Christ?' This influence works into people's lives in both the formal and the informal places of life; the accidental and the organised. Any parent will know that discipleship happens all around them in the messiness of everyday life, as young children quickly learn to mimic and take on the traits of their parents, whether we want them to or not! It is the combination of the organised and the accidental that is so powerful. The first disciples learned just as much by cooking breakfast with Jesus as they did by going on a ministry trip with him. Both are vital.

One of the powerful realities of discipleship, then, is that we learn in a variety of ways and settings, which God has designed for our growth and maturity. The gospels show us that the process by which Jesus discipled his followers was not uniform and that not everyone had the same access and relational proximity to Jesus at the same moment in time. He used all the vehicles of discipleship at his disposal; Jesus understood proxemics before it was even a word in the dictionary.

The theory of proxemics was first coined about fifty years ago by the social scientist Edward T. Hall, who investigated how the different uses of space in our lives play a role in our interpersonal communication.[7] He identified four key spaces around us that define the way we interact with one another in our daily lives and labelled them the intimate, personal, social and public spaces. Nineteen centuries earlier, Jesus helped his disciples to grow by using these four spaces, each of which has particular strengths and opportunities unique to its size.

### The Intimate Space (1–2 people)

The unique characteristic of intimate space discipleship is the closeness and vulnerability of relationship involved. Typically, these are one-on-one relationships with a high level of trust and are reserved for only a very few people over the course of our lives. Marriage partners and close friends are typical examples.

Jesus seems to have had a relationship like this with 'the disciple whom Jesus loved' (John 13:23), who is traditionally understood to have been the apostle John, the only one of the gospel writers to have described himself in such a way. I love that John knew the reality of Jesus' love for him so clearly, that he decided to put it in his gospel account as his own nickname! The apostle Paul's relationship with young Timothy is another great example of discipleship that happens in the intimate space of life; he called Timothy 'my true son in the faith' (1 Timothy 1:2,18; Philippians 2:19–22) and wrote with him letters that are now part of the New Testament. They served the same churches together, shared long and dangerous journeys, were imprisoned together and worshipped in the same prison cells, and Timothy was even circumcised at the hands of Paul. Ouch! Discipleship like this is about deep friendship, closeness, fathering and long-term commitment.

## The Personal Space (3–10 people)

The unique characteristic of personal space discipleship is being in a group that is small enough to build meaningful loving friendships and have mutual accountability, high commitment and a high degree of challenge. Luke records this of Jesus: 'When morning came, he called his disciples to him and chose twelve of them' (Luke 6:13). Mark adds that Jesus' purpose in drawing out twelve from the larger body of disciples was that they 'might be with him and that he might send them out to preach' (Mark 3:14).

The twelve disciples had unique access to Jesus in the first ever New Testament small group! They experienced discipleship unique to this personal space of learning and it was the context for their apostolic training.

Over the years, I have loved being in groups of this size, growing myself and helping others grow; it is honestly one of the most rewarding experiences in life to see others flourish in these settings. I'll never forget as a young man being part of midweek discipleship groups that were always a beautiful mixture of teenage chaos and heavenly glory! Evenings spent driving around looking for the best milkshake in the city, kicking a football around, opening the Bible and prophesying over one another – such evenings live long in the memory, because they were moments of huge transformation in my life. I grew because of leaders who intentionally and sacrificially poured out their Wednesday evenings in pursuit of raising some world changers.

## The Social Space (20–50 people)

The unique characteristic of social space discipleship is that it happens in a larger context and is big enough to have a missional impact with those who don't yet know Jesus. In the social space friendships can still form, though not to the same depth as in a smaller setting, and a strong sense of common purpose, shared goals and values creates an environment in which people come together to learn and make an impact. Typically, social space discipleship happens in classroom-based training settings.

Jesus made use of this size setting to great effect: 'He went down with them and stood on a level place. A large crowd of his disciples was there and a great number of people from all over Judea, from Jerusalem, and from the coastal region around Tyre and Sidon' (Luke 6:17). We don't know how large the crowd was on this occasion, but it necessitated Jesus standing on a level place to be heard. On another occasion, Jesus specifically sent out the 72 to bring the kingdom to surrounding towns and villages. Social space discipleship emphasises the vital elements of being part of a bigger community, being on mission together and being equipped to extend the kingdom.

## The Public Space (50+ people)

The unique characteristic of public space discipleship is the opportunity to cast vision, inspire and create a corporate momentum through shared encounters that you only get by being in a larger setting. Humans are hardwired to want to belong to something bigger than themselves. It is one of the ways that gifts and passions get ignited within us. The feeding of the 5,000 happened in the context of a very large gathering, where Jesus was teaching and preaching. It was the context for a shared experience of the miraculous in-breaking of God's kingdom. I am sure those who ate their miracle lunch that day talked about it for the rest of their lives! It was discipleship on a mass scale, as they were exposed to public ministry gifts that brought them into an encounter with the power and reality of God's presence.

Discipleship happens in all four of these spaces in our lives and, in the context of the church, we must be aware of the opportunities presented by them all. Discipleship is not uniform, but happens in the accidental and the organised, in the intimate and the public spaces of life. Ultimately, though, it is the influence of people that creates a lasting impact on our lives. What will we do with the influence God has given us?

Our encouragement is that you will read this discipleship manual not as a consumer, but as a participant. We pray that you will be inspired to join the ancient and joyful pursuit of becoming a disciple-making disciple of Jesus Christ, multiplying kingdom life wherever you go. It's time for a discipleship revolution, where we dare greatly in order to raise up multitudes of fully devoted followers of Jesus. Making disciples is the most rewarding, exhilarating, challenging, demanding, risky, worthwhile, scary but ultimately fulfilling pursuit you could throw your energy into. Don't stand on the sidelines. Get onto the pitch. Use your influence for something that will last forever. Go and make disciples!

It is not the critic who counts; not the man who points out how the strong man stumbles, or where the doer of deeds could have done them better. The credit belongs to the man who is actually in the arena, whose face is marred by dust and sweat and blood; who strives valiantly; who errs, who comes short again and again, because there is no effort without error and shortcoming; but who does actually strive to do the deeds; who knows great enthusiasms, the great devotions; who spends himself in a worthy cause; who at the best knows in the end the triumph of high achievement, and who at the worst, if he fails, at least fails while daring greatly, so that his place shall never be with those cold and timid souls who know neither victory nor defeat.[8]

# Foundations and Framework of Discipleship

It is vital that we have a clearly defined foundation and framework for discipleship. This defines our *what* and our *how*; *foundations* are concerned with *what* we are building and frameworks with *how* we build. Without these, it is all too easy to be blown here and there by every new idea, trend or fad, useful as these can sometimes be. Instead, a clearly defined foundation and framework facilitate the emergence of a naturally multiplying movement of disciples who know what they are doing and how to do it!

The following eight terms define a core operating system for any multiplying disciple, which means we nurture Christ-followers from a position of biblical and practical strength.

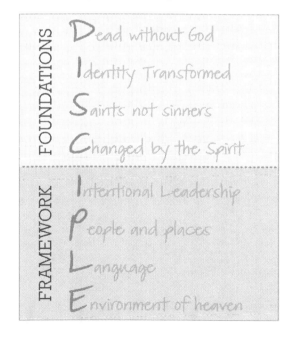

FOUNDATIONS

Dead without God

Identity Transformed

Saints not sinners

Changed by the Spirit

FRAMEWORK

Intentional Leadership

People and places

Language

Environment of heaven

## Foundations of Discipleship

**Dead without God:** Being a follower of Jesus starts when we admit that we are dead! Dead in our sin without Jesus and deserving to fall under God's judgement. It is not rule-keeping that makes us disciples of Jesus but his grace (which is a free gift) as we repent (which means to change our thinking) and follow him (Ephesians 2:1–9). We can't start in our discipleship until our thinking is clear on who we are without God.

*Have you fully realised how dead and hopeless you were without Jesus? What difference does it make to you, knowing you are saved and transformed by God's grace?*

**Identity transformed:** Our identity used to be based on family background, education, race, physical attributes or other things. But because of what Jesus has done we have been given a new identity for free. The life we now live we live by faith in Jesus (Galatians 2:20). It is through faith we understand that we are now radically loved by God and that he has defined us as anointed, walking in authority, adopted into his family, ambassadors for him, part of a royal priesthood and heavenly citizens. Realising this identity change is foundational to being a disciple as our behaviour follows from our beliefs.

*Are you living in the good of your new identity in Christ?*

**Saints not sinners:** When Jesus died on the cross, we died 'in him' and so we are now dead to sin and alive to God. We are no longer sinners who occasionally do the right thing, but saints who occasionally sin. This means that we fight sin not by trying harder but by first recognising that sinful behaviour is no longer what we naturally do. Discipleship is not self-help; God rescues and empowers us! One of the outward signs of this inward change is **baptism in water**, that all believers are commanded to do (Acts 2:38). Baptism symbolises dying to our old sinful life (under the water) and being raised with Christ in a new life as saints (coming out of the water).

*How does the realisation that you are dead to sin affect your approach to discipleship? Have you been baptised in water as a believer?*

**Changed by the Spirit:** Disciples are those who have been changed and are being changed through the power and work of the Holy Spirit. Receiving the Holy Spirit is the experience of being filled with God's power and life so that we can follow and love him effectively and joyfully (Acts 1:8). Being filled with the Spirit happens as we ask God to come and fill us (Ephesians 5:18). The Holy Spirit loves to breathe life into us so that we experience the fruit of being connected to him (Galatians 5:22) and the gifts that he gives us with which to serve him (1 Corinthians 12:8–11; Romans 12:6–8). The Holy Spirit enables the ongoing process of transformation to happen in our lives.

*Have you received the Holy Spirit and been filled with his power for living as a disciple of Jesus? What difference does this make in your life?*

# Framework of Discipleship

**Intentional leadership:** 'Go and make disciples of all nations' (Matthew 28:19). It is important that we are intentional in our discipling relationships. Disciples are called to be rivers, not swamps or deserts. Swamps typically have an inflow of water but nowhere for the water to go; deserts have an absence of inflow altogether. By contrast, rivers have water flowing both in and out, which is why they bring life! We are on this journey together and Jesus is looking for those who are continually receiving and giving away. We, therefore, need to be intentional in both joining and drawing others into discipling relationships.

*Have you taken responsibility for your discipleship? Who are you giving away to?*

**People and places:** 'Jesus went up on a mountainside and called to him those he wanted, and they came to him. He appointed twelve that they might be with him' (Mark 3:13–14). Discipleship, at its heart, is about working out relationships with the right people in the right places. Jesus worked out discipleship in groups of varying sizes from very large to very small. Similarly our discipling of others will take place in various sized communities; from one-on-one to the whole church gathering together. We need to make every effort to find, contribute to, and serve people in these different groups because this is how we learn and grow.

*Are you part of a community in the church where you are growing and have real friendships? Which size group is important for you in this season of your life?*

**Language in common:** Jesus used parables to communicate God's message in a memorable way to those who were hungry for truth (Matthew 13:10–17). In a similar way, we use a common language for our discipleship where clear principles are shown in a way that is easy to remember, understand and pass on to others. A common spiritual language helps us to make disciples who make disciples who make disciples! Learning a common language takes time but the effort more than makes up for itself when we are able to train and release others more effectively.

*Which parts of the language have you mastered already? What's the next step for you?*

**Environment of heaven:** 'Teaching them to obey everything I have commanded you' (Matthew 28:20). Jesus' words and commands create heavenly culture and our discipleship reflects our culture as a church family. It is to be honouring (identity based, reflecting each person's value to God), authentic (vulnerable, confidential), accepting (a judgement- and lecture-free atmosphere), generous (of time and resources) and courageous (speaking the truth in love, sharing with those who don't know Christ).

*How is the culture reflected in the discipling relationships that you are part of?*

LEARNING TO LIVE LIKE JESUS

UP
Connection

OUT
Calling

IN
Character &
Community

## PLAY:
### Learning to Live Like Jesus

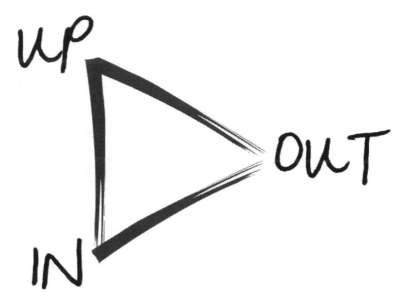

### The three-dimensional rhythm for all healthy disciples

The disciple of Jesus has a healthy blend of UP, IN and OUT in their life. Jesus said to his first disciples, 'Follow me and I will make you fishers of men' (Matthew 4:19). This was Jesus' commitment to his disciples: to connect them to himself ('follow me'), transform their characters in community ('and I will make you') and launch them onto his mission to transform the world around them ('fishers of men').

## UP (Connection): Exalt, Enjoy and Encounter

UP is about our connection to God. Looking up involves *exalting* God for his greatness, *enjoying* God for his goodness and *encountering* God in his glory. The primary call of any disciple is to love God and walk with him. It is in this place of worship, adoration, friendship and pursuit of him that life and fruitfulness flow into the life of any disciple. Learning how to pray, to read the Bible, to hear God's voice and encounter him in worship are the mainstays of the *upward* life of a child of God.

## IN (Character and Community): Ideas, Identity and Behaviour

IN is about the development of our character. This always happens in the context of community. Looking in involves changing our *ideas* (world view and thoughts) to line up with the Bible, understanding our new *identity* in Christ and for that truth to transform our *behaviour* accordingly. God is happily committed to transforming our lives to look like Jesus; this is the process of character development. Key to this process is that God puts us into a community called the church; in order to grow in character we need other people. Very little change happens in a box; we need others! Forgiveness, love, honour and encouragement can only flow when we are in real relationships where love and truth can bring about maturity (Ephesians 4:15). Key tools for our character development include understanding God's big picture, walking in repentance, learning how to stay healthy and living in our new identity as children of God.

## OUT (Calling): Ministry, Mission and Multiplication

OUT is about fulfilling our calling. Looking out involves nurturing our *ministry* gifts, being on *mission* with Jesus and *multiplying* disciples as we seek to see his kingdom extended. Jesus did not enlist his disciples to a cruise-liner but a battleship! Jesus has commissioned each of us to bring hope, courage, promise and joy wherever we find ourselves. We are rivers not swamps, releasing the overflow of all God has freely given us. The *outward* life involves understanding our ministry motivations, what God has called us to do with our lives, how to bring the kingdom of God and how to multiply and make disciples.

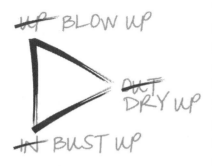

This is what a balanced Jesus-shaped discipleship looks like: a healthy rhythm and blend of the UP, the IN and the OUT. Without the presence of all three aspects in our lives we can easily begin to miss God's best for us. If we have no *upward* focus we can easily BLOW UP because sustaining power for life is only found in connection with God. If we have no *inward* focus, we can easily BUST UP because we need strong character worked out in community to truly grow and thrive. If we have no *outward* focus, we can easily DRY UP, because every good thing God gives us is made to be given away freely to others and especially to those who do not yet know Jesus.

**Key Questions:**

Which area of UP, IN and OUT are you strongest in at the moment? Why?

Which area of UP, IN and OUT needs more attention in your life at the moment?

**Additional Resources:**

Watch: *How to Use the Play Symbol Tutorial* kingsarms.org/play

UP
Connection

OUT
Calling

IN
Character &
Community

CONNECTION (UP):
Exalt, Enjoy and Encounter

# POWER:

## Power up and start with prayer

Sonship
Thanks
Ask
Repent
Truth

### Praying using the Lord's Prayer in Luke 11:2–10

Power for life comes when we start with prayer because talking and listening to God plugs us into his love, will and life. The more we encounter him in personal prayer, the more we become like him. Beholding enables becoming. Developing a lifestyle of personal prayer was modelled by Jesus who sought to find a regular time and place in his busy life to connect with the Father (Mark 1:35; Matthew 6:6).

Jesus taught his disciples about the content of his prayer life in what we know as the Lord's Prayer (Luke 11:2–10). It shows us five key ingredients for a healthy and enjoyable prayer time. Using the acronym START, we can pray as follows.

## S = Sonship: 'Our Father in heaven' (v2)

Begin by thanking God that he is your Father and you are his child. Spend time meditating on your amazing Father and your new identity as his child (Luke 15:11–31; Romans 8:14–16).

## T = Thanks and Honour: 'Hallowed be your name' (v2)

Hallowed means God's name is honoured above all others. Spend time worshipping him for who he is and thank him for all that he has done (Psalm 145; Psalm 18; Ephesians 1:3–14; Revelation 7:9–11).

## A = Ask: 'Your kingdom come . . . and give us this day' (v2–3)

Spend time asking God to bring breakthrough in the world around you, the lives of those you love and in your own life. Ask that his kingdom will fill the earth and that he meets your personal needs (Acts 4:29–30; Isaiah 61:1–4; Ephesians 3:14–21).

## R = Repent and Forgive: 'Forgive us . . . we forgive . . . deliver us' (v4)

Spend time asking for and giving forgiveness and for the ability to overcome temptation, evil and to overcome the enemy (Psalm 103:8–12; Matthew 6:14; Ephesians 4:31–32; 1 John 1:9).

## T = Truth: 'Ask and it will be given to you' (v9–10)

Finish your prayer time by declaring the truth about God – he is a good

Father who loves to answer you because he is good and listens to your prayers (John 15:7; 1 John 5:14; Romans 8:28; Romans 8:31–39; Psalm 136:1–6).

---

**Key Questions:**

What are you thanking God for at the moment?

How have you seen God answer your prayers in the past?

What are you asking God for at the moment?

Decide on some prayer goals for the next few months: how often you want to pray, who you want to pray with, what you want to pray for.

---

**Additional Resources:**

Read: Dutch Sheets, *Intercessory Prayer* (Regal Books, 2008)

Read: Pete Greig and Dave Roberts, *Red Moon Rising* (Kingsway Publications, 2004)

Listen: Phil Wilthew, *Devotion Part 1 on Prayer* kingsarms.org/prayertalk

# View from the Front Line: Disciples Who Pray

I have been learning how to pray for around 24 years and I am still learning. While I grew up in a Christian home and was very familiar with having times of prayer, it was not until my early teenage years that I began to develop my own relationship with God and use the Lord's Prayer as my template for relating to him.

Jesus instructs us that when we pray we should go to a private place, shut the door and seek our Father who is unseen. As a rather self-conscious teenager, the most secret prayer-space I could think of was the shower. Most evenings, music blaring to avoid my voice being overheard, I would hop into the shower and rather falteringly set off on the journey of learning how to talk to my heavenly Father. Jesus says that when we prioritise seeking God in the unseen places of our lives, our Father will reward us. In other words, unseen realities are impacted by our unseen priorities. In the spiritual realm of life, what we do in private becomes spiritual capital and heavenly currency. This is what caused Sidlow Baxter to say, 'Men may spurn our appeals, reject our message, oppose our arguments, despise our persons, but they are helpless against our prayers.'[9]

Prayer with the living God, like building any meaningful relationship, is a process that takes time and is one that I am very much still growing in. Sometimes, even now, I fall asleep when praying; at other times, I find my mind wandering onto all manner of things, other than what I am actually meant to be doing. I still find that words don't always come easy and I'm not quite sure what to say. At times, more sleep can seem so much more appealing than more prayer. But I am learning. And the key thing is this – the only way to learn how to pray, is to actually pray. No textbook, neat methodology or someone else's story can really teach you what you need to know most. Start to pray. It's the only way!

Charles Spurgeon once said, 'I would rather teach one man to pray than ten men to preach.' Sitting behind Spurgeon's logic was perhaps the understanding that prayer is what really changes us. When we pray, we cannot guarantee that all the things we petition God for will be answered in exactly the way that we hope, but we can always guarantee that prayer will change us, because proximity to God cannot fail but to make us more like him. Ultimately, we always become like the one we behold.

I'll never forget once listening to a visiting American pastor, Dee Duke, who relayed to us his usual marriage counselling practice for those in need of his pastoral help. His stock advice to struggling couples was simple: 'Before I will agree to see you, you need to agree that for the next two weeks you will both commit to praying together for at least thirty seconds every day. If you still have a problem after that, you can come back and see me.' He reported that 90 per cent of those who followed his advice needed no further counselling but found their marriages enriched, transformed and revived by God's presence in prayer. Prayer does change circumstances because it fundamentally changes us. Prayer is critical to discipleship.

Martin Luther, the great 16th-century German reformer, is reported to have said that he had so much business that he could not get by with less than 3 hours of daily prayer. In my more legalistic and easily condemned days, the main challenge I felt from that statement was that I clearly was not praying long or hard enough. I have now come to realise the main issue is not about the minutes but the mind-set. When I'm with Jesus, I bear fruit. I am meant to live as a dependent disciple. Apart from regular, daily, life-giving prayer connection with Jesus, I can do nothing. Luther understood that our fruitfulness depends on being with him.

Fundamentally, this is why Jesus' first disciples came to him asking for coaching, because they could see the connection between his private life with the Father and his public life of power.

Prayer is a relationship, not a ritual, which is why prayer began in the Garden of Eden before there were any breakthroughs to be obtained, crises to avert or needs to meet. Prayer starts with God and mankind walking together in the cool of the day, enjoying the beauty of friendship in sinless paradise. It is for this reason that Jesus coaches us to start prayer by remembering our sonship, God's fatherhood and our enjoyment of a God who is so utterly captivating and majestic.

One of the practical ways our family would power up and start to pray in this way was by playing the A-B-C prayer game around the dinner table in the evenings, especially when our children were younger. Each of us would take a turn to thank God for something that we loved about him, working our way through the letters of the alphabet. 'God, thank you that you are Amazing, thank you that you are Beautiful, thank you that you are Creative,' and so on. I admit, the letters Q and X always needed a bit of creative licence, but I think we can all agree that God is Quintessentially majestic and Xcellent in all his ways!

Another critical part of my own journey in learning to be a disciple who prays, has been to learn by praying with other people. Luke 9:18 says that one day Jesus was praying in private and that his disciples were with him. It sounds very much like the kind of privacy you uniquely get to enjoy as a parent of very small children, where no space is sacred anymore – wherever you go, they follow! Jesus' disciples learnt to pray by seeing Jesus pray and listening to him. If you want to learn to be a disciple who prays, spend time with others who pray.

One of the men I respect most in the world has a simple approach to discipleship. As a prominent church movement leader and Bible teacher he was never short of people who wanted his coaching and input, but his answer was almost always the same: 'Come and pray with me.' Those who took that invitation received the best education possible, because when you get around people who know God in prayer, you learn, grow and transform.

John Nelson Hyde was an American missionary to the Punjab early in the 20th century, who affectionately became known as Praying Hyde, such was his passion for prayer. Partially deaf and struggling to learn the dialect of his new adopted home, Hyde decided he would give himself to prayer in order to change the world. At a prayer convention in 1908 he asked God to give him one new follower of Jesus a day and committed to pray day and night for its realisation. By the end of that first year, he had seen 400 make a decision to follow Christ. He doubled his prayer target for the following year and saw a further 800 make a response in 1909. This number doubled again the following year until a whole unreached people group found itself in the grip of a new move of God.

One man who prayed with Hyde described his prayer-education in the following way:

> He came to my room, turned the key in the door, dropped on his knees, waited five minutes without a single syllable coming from his lips. I could hear my own heart thumping and beating. I felt the hot tears running down my face. I knew I was with God. Then with upturned face, down which the tears were streaming, he said: 'Oh, God!' Then for five minutes at least, he was still again, and then when he knew he was talking with God his arm went around my shoulder and there came up from the depth of his heart such petitions for men as I had never heard before. I rose from my knees to know what real prayer was.[10]

Praying with others can be one of the most life-changing experiences. My wife was worshipping God and praying in our bedroom one day.

She had headphones on, worship music going and was so lost in the moment that she stood at the window, eyes closed, arms aloft in exultation and wonder, and failed to notice the window cleaner climbing up his ladder on the other side of the glass. When she opened her eyes, the two of them shared a startled moment that I would pay good money to go back and see! That window cleaner received an accidental education that day on how to pray, but you can deliberately seek out men and women to do this journey with. It will change you!

It's never too late to power up and start to pray, because prayer is a journey of discovery with a God who loves you and wants to pour out blessing on the world around you, through your prayers. As Martin Luther is reported to have said, 'Prayer is not about overcoming God's reluctance, but laying hold of his willingness.' It's time to power up and start to pray!

# STOP:

## Stop and read the word

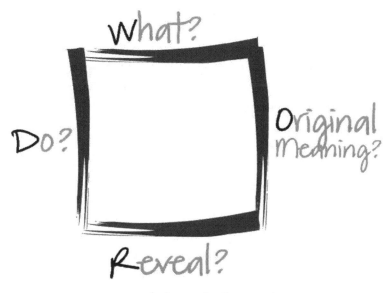

What?

Original meaning?

Do?

Reveal?

## Getting to know God through the Bible

The Bible is one of God's gifts to help us connect with him in a deeper way and is described as 'alive and active' (Hebrews 4:12), 'flawless' (Psalm 18:30) and is all about Jesus (John 5:39). Digging into the Bible is an important aspect of getting to know God and is essential for training ourselves to be more like him (2 Timothy 3:16).

When you read the Bible, you will find it helpful to stop and ask the following four questions about God's WORD:

## W = What does it say?

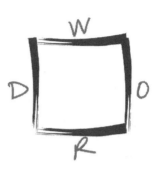

Reading the Bible starts with loving what God has to say. Disciples have a love and hunger for the truth of God's word found in the Bible. It's good to start by simply reading the passage. What do you think it is saying? Ask the Holy Spirit for revelation and use different translations of the Bible – English Standard Version (ESV), New Living Translation (NLT) or New International Version (NIV) for example – to help you grapple with its meaning.

## O = Observations

Next, ask yourself: What observations can I make about this passage? What stands out to me from what I have just read? What might the hearers of the time have understood by the events recorded? Is there anything that I don't immediately understand, and that I need to find out more about? How does this passage connect to other parts of the Bible? The best Bible study is done in the context of hunger to find out more and to know God in the process.

Three tools to use in observation are:

**Context:** Use the 20/20 rule – if you don't understand the passage you are reading, try reading twenty verses before and twenty verses after it to understand the context better.

**Community:** It is also useful for us to grasp what the Bible means through talking to one another in our church family. Community life is a great way to learn what the Bible actually means as we discuss and share with each other.

**Commentaries:** Bible commentaries and online tools can help shed more light on the scripture we are reading.

### R = Reveal about God or Me

What does this passage show about the nature of God or about yourself? What truth does it reveal to you? Does it challenge or expose any misconceptions in your understanding, any lies that you've been believing about God, others or yourself? Ask the Spirit to speak to you.

### D = Do

What are you going to do with what you have read? How does it affect what you believe? Are there any decisions you need to make or actions you need to take? How does this truth apply in your daily life and how will you remember to do it?

---

**Key Questions:**

What are you reading in the Bible at the moment?

What is God speaking to you about through what you are reading?

How is what you're reading changing your thinking?

What do you need to start doing, stop doing or do differently as a result of what you have read?

---

**Additional Resources:**

Visit kingsarms.org/bioy for resources and links to online commentaries and reading plans

Read: Gordon Fee and Douglas Stuart, *How to Read the Bible for All Its Worth* (Zondervan, 2003)

Read: Vaughan Roberts, *God's Big Picture: Tracing the Storyline of the Bible* (IVP, 2003)

# View From the Front Line: Disciples Who Read the Bible

One night I began to dream. In the dream I was having a conversation with a friend who was looking at a Bible in my hand. The friend asked me, 'How much is your Bible worth?' Answering quite literally, I looked at the book in my hand and said, 'About £30. How much was yours?' My friend looked me in the eyes and simply replied, 'Mine is priceless!' I awoke with a fresh sense of conviction from God that, as a disciple of Jesus, I must value the Bible for the priceless gift it is to me from God.

The Bible, which simply means 'writings', is a library of 66 books, written on 3 continents over a period of about 1,000 years by around 40 authors using 3 languages – namely, Hebrew, Aramaic and Greek. It contains a variety of genres, including historical narrative, poetry, prophecy, biography and letters, and is divided into two parts that we call the Old and New Testaments. The 39 books of the Old Testament date from before the time of Jesus; the 27 books of the New Testament date from the time of Jesus onwards. The Bible is one of the most breathtaking all-time best-sellers on the planet, having sold nearly 4 billion copies in the last 50 years alone, more than any other book. It is God's authoritative word on his nature, his plans and his ways, and is the guidebook for every disciple.

The Bible itself testifies to its living authority, saying, 'We also thank God continually because, when you received the word of God, which you heard from us, you accepted it not as a word, but as it actually is, the word of God' (1 Thessalonians 2:13).

Likewise, Paul reminds his friend Timothy, 'All scripture is God-breathed and is useful for teaching, rebuking, correcting and training in righteousness, so that the servant of God may be thoroughly equipped for every good work' (2 Timothy 3:16–17). 'Scripture' also means 'writings' and is another word for the Bible.

Both these verses tell us that the Bible is more than a collection of ancient writings or interesting historical texts. Scripture is the very word of God, described elsewhere as 'alive and active. Sharper than a double-edged sword' (Hebrews 4:12). Scripture lives because God lives and the words that come from his mouth carry and contain the same power and authority as when he first uttered them.

As a young boy I suffered from vivid nightmares for many years, often waking several times a night, having seen terrifying things in my sleep. I remember often sitting at the top of the stairs, weeping and crying out for my parents, who would often take me into their own bed until I fell asleep and could be carried back to my own. Despite all their best efforts, nothing really seemed to shift whatever was bothering my night-time hours. That was, until the words of a particular scripture arrowed into my heart like a message sent directly from God.

My mum came home one day and shared a verse from the Psalms that simply said: 'In peace I will lie down and sleep, for you alone, LORD, make me dwell in safety' (Psalm 4:8). As I read it, I felt faith leap in my heart; I wrote it down and hung it above my bed, memorising the verse and repeating it to myself. From that moment, the nightmares stopped as a superior truth gripped my heart and mind. God was bigger than my fears! I was safe! In many ways, I was walking through our discipleship tool, 'Stop and read the word', without realising it: I had understood what it said (W); made my own observations that God would look after me (O); seen a revelation that I need not fear (R); and made the decision (D) to trust the God who inspired those words. It was truly life-changing.

Because God's word is so life-transforming, disciples of Jesus take seriously the call to be diligent students and readers of scripture.

This can take many forms, from daily reading plans, working through particular books of the Bible, using Bible commentary tools or using online resources. Whatever you do, do it regularly and do it often. Reading the Bible is like eating regular meals. You may not remember exactly what you ate for lunch five days ago, but it is still doing your body good, providing necessary strength and sustenance. Reading scripture is a profoundly spiritual exercise. It renews the mind, washes the soul, refreshes the spirit, often in unseen ways, which, if done regularly, will strengthen and sustain your life as a disciple. You don't need to remember (or immediately understand) everything you read, but as you digest it with faith, humility and hunger, it will begin to shape your attitudes, desires and priorities in a God-centred way that will stun you!

Taking the decision to stop and read the word of God in my life has led to many moments of encounter and life change. I'll never forget reading through the books of Jeremiah, Isaiah and Ezekiel in my first year at university and being gripped by God's righteousness and heart for justice. It changed me. I'll never forget memorising the stunning summary of God's grace in the first half of Ephesians 1 and praying through it day by day, line by line. It changed me. I'll never forget walking through a tough season where I was battling feelings of deep anger and unforgiveness towards someone and wanted revenge: God spoke to me one day from the book of Job, which said, 'Beware of turning to evil, which you seem to prefer to affliction' (Job 36:21). When I read those words, I wept with repentance. It changed me.

When we stop and read the Bible, it is vital we remember that there is a big story being told through all 66 books. The Bible is organised more like a library than a chronological story, especially in the Old Testament. However, whether you are reading the history section, the law section, the poetry or the prophetic writings, they tell one unified story and it is the story of Jesus.

Jesus was in conversation one day with the religious leaders of his time, who knew the Scriptures like the backs of their hands and would have committed to memory the majority of the 39 books of the Old Testament. Yet to these men, who opposed him, Jesus said:

'You study the Scriptures diligently because you think that in them you have eternal life. These are the very Scriptures that testify about me, yet you refuse to come to me to have life.' (John 5:39–40)

Unless we read the Bible with the understanding that Jesus is the central character, we miss the point, because it all leads to him. The Bible is essentially a story of love and war. God, the creator, loved us, but we went to war with him by rejecting him. So God went to war against our sinfulness, sickness, rebellion and ensuing separation from him. He sent his own beloved son, Jesus, to be our substitute and our saviour, paying the price of our wrongdoing to win us back. From the beginning of the story to the end, Jesus is the central character: he is the promised Saviour-King of the Old Testament; he is the present Saviour-King of the New Testament; and he is the future Saviour-King of eternity. It's all about Jesus. It's time to stop and read his word.

# RECORD:

Record the prophetic

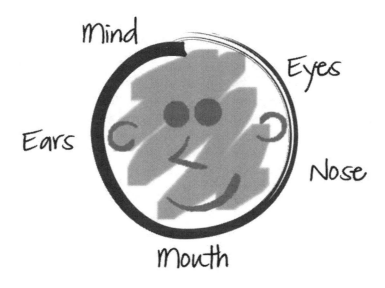

mind

Eyes

Ears

Nose

mouth

Five ways we hear the voice of God

God speaks today and hearing his voice is a vital part of our friendship with him and worship of him. Jesus says that we are called to live by 'every word that comes from the mouth of God' (Matthew 4:4). God speaks to each of us differently because we hear him out of our unique relationship with him and the unique way that he has made us.

The Holy Spirit always speaks in a way that glorifies Jesus, honours scripture and encourages his people. Using the record button, consider the following five ways we can tune in and capture what he is saying.

**The Eyes:** We hear God as we see what he says through the Bible (2 Timothy 3:16) and we can also see visions, pictures and images that have spiritual meanings and direction (Acts 2:17; Jeremiah 1:11–13; Acts 16:9). The Bible is, in fact, the vital ingredient in all the ways we hear God's voice, as it provides a framework against which all other revelation is measured, and within which it finds its meaning and context. God will never contradict what he has caused to be written in the Bible, and anything we believe we've heard from him will be consistent with it.

**The Mind:** We hear God as we remember with our minds what he has done and as he inspires our thoughts, dreams and imaginations (1 Corinthians 2:9 – 10:16; Acts 2:17; Daniel 1:17; Romans 12:2).

**The Ears:** We hear God's voice through the words we hear, with our physical ears or spiritual senses. Often his words come as flashing thoughts, sentences or single words of revelation (John 10:27; Jeremiah 33:3; John 16:13; Isaiah 30:21).

**The Mouth:** We hear him through the words we speak, inspired by the Holy Spirit in the moment we speak them as well as receiving revelation from the counsel of others (Matthew 10:19–20; Proverbs 1:5, 15:22).

**The Nose:** God can speak to us through all our senses, our gut instincts and intuitions. We sense and feel that he is present in situations and places (Job 38:36; Job 32:8; 1 Corinthians 2:11).

The Bible teaches that we are not to despise prophecy but instead test it and hold on to the good (1 Thessalonians 5:21).

There are three stages in holding onto the good and applying what God has said:

- Observation – What did you see, hear or observe?

- Interpretation – What do you think it means?

- Application – What should you do?

There are also three ways in which we can test or weigh something we believe God has said:

First, we check that it is consistent with the teaching of the Bible. God will never contradict what he has already said and caused to be written down in scripture.

Second, we check that it is encouraging, strengthening or comforting (1 Corinthians 14:3). New Testament prophecy builds up, cheers up and lifts up. It never brings condemnation, even if God is calling us to change our attitudes or habits. It draws people to Jesus and calls out the best in them.

Third, we talk to other Christians, preferably those who have experience of hearing God themselves. God has put us in community so that we can draw wisdom and strength from one another. Ask others what they think of what you feel you have heard from God.

Applying these stages and testing that the prophecy is in line with God's word is crucial to growing in hearing his voice.

**Key Questions:**

How do you hear from God?

What specific way of hearing from God would you like to grow in? Identify someone who can help you with this.

What is God saying to you and what are you going to do about it?

How are you recording what God says to you? If you aren't yet, think of a way to start.

In what ways do you 'weigh' what you feel God is saying?

**Additional Resources:**

Read: Julian C. Adams, *Gaining Heaven's Perspective* (River Publishing, 2012)

Read: Jack Deere, *Surprised by the Voice of God* (Kingsway Publications, 2006)

Read: Jack Deere, *The Beginner's Guide to the Gift of Prophecy* (Regal Books, 2009)

# View From the Front Line: Disciples Who Hear God

Jesus is the great Shepherd and his sheep recognise his voice (John 10:4). It is your inheritance to hear your God's voice but, as with any relationship, it takes time to learn someone else's language. God speaks in spiritual words that are spiritually discerned, and hearing him is an art that only comes through friendship, listening, understanding and time. What is critical for disciples of Jesus is that we develop a deep hunger to hear him speak.

One evening, when my children were much younger, the supervising of teeth cleaning was carrying on much as it always did, when quite out of the blue a God encounter happened. My then six-year-old son Sam suddenly blurted out through toothpaste-coated teeth, 'Dad, God never speaks to me. I can't hear him!' I began to explain to Sam that we can all hear God's voice; we just need to learn how to listen. I began to teach him some of the different ways that God speaks to us, including the five ways mentioned in this discipleship tool. I asked, 'Sam, shall we ask God to speak to you now?' He nodded, sat himself down on the toilet seat, closed his eyes and concentrated very hard. I explained that I would ask the Holy Spirit to show him a picture and that he should tell me as soon as an image came into his mind.

We prayed and, sure enough, God gave him a picture of me praying in my bedroom. 'That's awesome, Sam,' I responded. 'Now, what do you think God might be saying through that picture?' Sam shrugged his shoulders and said he didn't know, so we prayed again, this time asking God to show us the meaning of the picture. After just a few seconds, quick as a flash, Sam said to me, 'Dad, I think God wants you to pray more!'

Not only was it a very humorous moment, it was also a very accurate one. God had spoken, simply yet profoundly, through my six-year-old son, purely because he took time to listen and learn. Learning how to listen is a big deal for any disciple.

When God speaks to us in these kinds of ways, we need to ask ourselves three questions:

- What is God saying?

- What does it mean?

- What should I do about it?

These are the questions of *revelation*, *interpretation* and *application*.

*Revelation* comes in many forms, as our tool details. It often happens that a person more easily hears God speak in a particular way, but God can communicate with us through all our senses, our mind and our emotions.

Some people are predominantly 'feelers', sensing in their emotions and spirits what God is saying, and receiving particular impressions, discernment or 'burdens'. If you are a 'feeler', you may be particularly sensitive to how other people are feeling and have a high degree of emotional empathy.

Others may predominantly be 'hearers', sensing what God is saying through words or phrases that drop into their minds. They will often sense God speaking words of knowledge to them about situations and physical sicknesses he wants to break into and heal. Hearers may often be used by God to prophesy over other people.

Some may also predominately discern God's voice through seeing. 'Seers' will tend to hear God through dreams, pictures and visual clues in the world around us.

*Interpretation* has to do with how we understand and make sense of the things that God has spoken. We don't always understand what we have seen, so it is important to ask the next question: what does this mean? Sometimes we need other people to help us in this process, particularly where God has spoken to us through dreams or pictures.

A friend of mine was helping to pray for guests on an Alpha Course at our church and his attention was especially drawn to one man sitting in the front row. As he began to ask God what he should pray for, he clearly felt God imprint the phrase, 'Alright, mate?' into his mind. Feeling somewhat sheepish about sharing such a strange word that seemed neither powerful nor profound, he nevertheless obeyed the prompting. Calling the man out, he said, 'I don't know if this makes any sense to you, but I feel God would simply say to you, "Alright, mate?"' At this point, the man's face lit up into a beaming smile and, soon afterwards, he gave his life to Christ. It transpired that the previous week he had gone home after the Alpha talk on prayer and for the very first time tried to pray on his own. Not having a religious background, he was somewhat unsure about how he should address the Almighty (or even, at this stage, whether the Almighty existed!), so he simply decided to talk to God like his friend and started with, 'Alright, God?' Unsure whether this was really the done thing, he then asked God to give him a sign that his prayer had been heard. When my friend shared his simple prophetic word, 'Alright, mate?' its meaning was immediately clear and led to a stunning encounter with Jesus.

*Application* is the last vital piece of the jigsaw, where we ask what we should do with what God has shown us. In a tense and dramatic moment, the apostle Paul received a prophetic word that he would be arrested and handed over to hostile officials in Jerusalem. Those around Paul immediately rushed to a faulty application, trying to persuade him to escape the danger by not going to Jerusalem; they assumed that they knew what to do with this revelation from God.

Paul, however, took a different view, saying, 'I am ready not only to be bound, but also to die in Jerusalem for the name of the Lord Jesus.' When he would not be dissuaded, his friends gave up and said, 'The Lord's will be done' (Acts 21:13–14). Paul knew that God was calling him into danger, not out of it, and was ready to enter the most hostile of environments because God had already told him, when he first became a disciple, that he would speak about Jesus to leaders and rulers and would suffer for Jesus' sake (Acts 9:16). This later prophecy was a powerful confirmation of God's earlier word to Paul, as he applied it correctly.

As we see, God may speak to other people through us. When telling someone what we think God is saying to them, it is really important to do so in a way that empowers, strengthens and encourages them. Unlike the Old Testament prophets, our words do not carry the authority of scripture but instead should be tested, talked about and shared with others so as to bring freedom, not control.

Here are the A-B-Cs of sharing prophetic words with others:

A: All about Jesus. Prophetic words should always give glory to Jesus and help us to love and connect with him more deeply.

B: Build up. Prophetic words for others should strengthen, encourage or comfort them, never dominate, discourage or frighten them.

C: Consistent with scripture. God has already given his authoritative word in the Bible. Our prophetic words must be in line with this original blueprint.

D: Delivered with love. Ultimately, if you hear God really accurately but have no love for people, you have missed God's heartbeat (1 Corinthians 13:2). Love is the motivation and the delivery system for the prophetic.

We were all born to hear God's voice, and disciples grow by listening to what he says. Years ago, when our church family was raising money for our first building purchase, a man felt he saw someone handing us a cheque with £146,000 on it. At the time, raising such a figure seemed out of the question. We were a small church and resources were limited. But when God speaks, faith rises: hearing God releases not only information, but impartation. On that first gift day, after all the gifts were counted, we had astonishingly raised £146,343. Hearing and receiving what God says changes lives and situations. Disciples of Jesus take seriously the call to record the prophetic.

# REFRESH:

Respond and refresh in worship

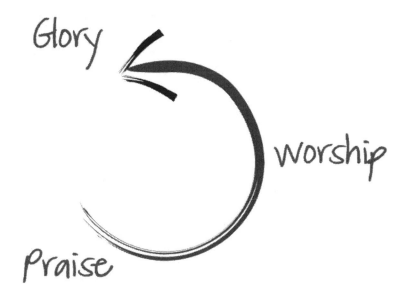

Glory

worship

Praise

Exalting and Enjoying God

Spending time in God's presence through worship is one of the great joys of our connection to God. Worship is not only a right response to God's goodness and glory but is also the most refreshing activity for the human soul.

Although worship describes our whole lives, it is also expressed in moments when we draw aside specifically to give honour and thanks to God. Worship is both a powerful individual response to who God is and an expression of our delight in him as a church community. We are called to be a people of worship! Whether we sing, pray or speak our worship, three ingredients will help us take steps towards standing and staying in God's presence, as so helpfully highlighted by Ruth Heflin in her book, *Glory: Experiencing the Atmosphere of Heaven.*[11]

This is not a worship formula, but a helpful reminder that our encounter with God has many different elements. **Psalm 24** is a helpful framework for this.

**Praise**

Psalm 24:1–2: Praise is a great starting place because it's the natural response to the revelation of who God is and what he has done for us. As Charles Spurgeon said, 'Christians are made to glorify God. We are never in our element until we are praising him.'[12] As you praise, it can involve some or all of the following expressions found in the Bible:

BOASTING: the word *hallelujah* means to boast, to celebrate (Psalm 113:1).

HANDS: we lift our hands in praise to the God who is above all worries, fears, hopes and dreams (Psalm 63:4).

THANKSGIVING: we express thanks for all he has done and who he is (Psalm 34:1–3).

DANCING: the Bible talks about dancing and celebrating with our bodies as an expression of our praise (Psalm 30:11–12). As we boast in the Lord, we often begin to draw near in more intimate worship.

## (Intimate) worship

Psalm 24:3–6: Intimate worship is where we enjoy the near presence of God and express our love for him. Typically, our focus shifts onto enjoying him and expressing desire for more of him in our lives. We encounter God's nearness, tenderness and love. Intimate worship is characterised by fewer words but heartfelt devotion, adoration and longing (John 4:23). It is a love response to God as saviour, friend and healer. It is about enjoying God and expressing our heart for him. As Richard Foster said, 'Worship is our response to the overtures of love from the heart of the Father.'[13]

## Standing in his glory

Psalm 24:7–10: The word for glory literally means 'weighty'; something so weighty that everything else has to shift around it. God's glory is his weighty and powerful presence. Whilst we know that God's presence is everywhere, the Bible is clear that he also loves to make his presence obvious to his people. The God who is everywhere loves to show up somewhere! Times in his glory can bring inner transformation, stunning revelation, the hearing of his voice with great clarity and moments of breakthrough in our lives. In the presence of his glory, anything could happen!

> **Key Questions:**
> How do you worship God in your own times with him?
> What can you do to increasingly connect your heart with God?

**Additional Resources:**

Read: Matt Redman, *Facedown* (Bethany House Publishers, 2012)

Read: J.I. Packer, *Knowing God* (Hodder & Stoughton, 2005)

# View From The Front Line: Disciples Who Worship

The Westminster Shorter Catechism, written in 1646, begins with the immortal statement: 'The chief end of man is to glorify God and to enjoy him forever.' In other words, we were born to worship. The only place where mankind truly finds rest is in the place of adoring, abandoned, passionate praise of the God who made us for his own glory and pleasure. Worship defines us because we always become like the one that we behold.

Worship describes the attitude of our whole lives and cannot be confined to sung worship in a church service. It involves our mind, body, priorities, attitudes, speech, work life, home life and everything else in between. I'll never forget the first time God asked me to give away a month's salary to help serve and support the work of planting churches in poorer nations. It felt like a crazy, reckless, extravagant thing to do, but that's what worship is. It is the decision to give ourselves wholly, fully, trustingly to the pursuit of the Saviour of our souls. I discovered on that occasion, and many times since, that you can never out-give the God of extravagant mercy. Worship has the habit of drawing us into wonder-working encounters with our Father. Worship involves all of life.

That said, worshipping God in scripture involves three key elements; namely, praise, worship and glory. While these three pieces of the worship jigsaw are not necessarily sequential, very often we find that the pursuit of the first piece leads to our experience and enjoyment of the others. It is not a formula, but often praise leads the journey into the intimate and glorious moments of wonder with the Lord. I believe the writers of the Westminster Shorter Catechism understood the connection between giving glory to God and enjoying him.

Praise is a delight and a discipline. There are moments where we cannot help but shout and declare the excellencies of God. Our hearts feel fit to burst and we cannot contain our boasting in the Lord. But there are other seasons when praise is a sacrifice that comes at a cost. I will never forget one of the worst mornings of my life. I was following my usual morning routine of walking the dog and spending some time with Jesus, and arrived home just in time to hear my wife answer a call from her brother with the worst of news. Carole's father had tragically and suddenly died that morning. The call ended and she collapsed on the floor as the world around us caved in with screams of pain and tears of loss. As we knelt in our front room, holding each other's shaking bodies, we made a decision: it was the decision to praise. We turned to Jesus and thanked him for his faithfulness, his grace, his strength and his wisdom.

Praise is our great defence and refuge, because when our hearts grow faint, there is a 'rock that is higher than I' (Psalm 61:2). As Rick Warren wrote after the tragic loss of his son, 'Oysters tenaciously attach to a ROCK larger than themselves. Then no punishing wave or violent storm can sweep them away.' Praise defines us, especially in seasons of mystery, loss, sacrifice and delay. Praise lifts us to the reality that matters more than any other – that God is on the throne and that he is faithful, loving and good.

There is also the beautiful intimacy we experience in worship that so often exists on the other side of our decisions to praise God. The word used most often in the New Testament for 'worship' means to 'kiss the feet' and has the connotations of both reverence and intimacy: I am bowing down to my superior, yet doing so in the knowledge that he is the one I love and who loves me. We worship in both the friendship and the fear of God.

My own experience of worship changed dramatically when a new lodger moved into my parents' home. Dave began to sing worship songs in his room, loud enough for all to hear. As I listened, it ignited something in my soul. I heard a man enjoying God and I wanted to do the same. Dave quickly taught me three chords on the guitar and I was off and running, learning how to draw near to God on my own. As I lost myself in worship, hours would fly by and at times Jesus' presence was so real and close that I felt sure he would be standing right in front of me if I opened my eyes.

When we worship, it is so important that we find the right vehicles of expression to connect our hearts with God. Depending on your temperament and personality, that could include all manner of things: reading a psalm from the Bible, painting a picture, writing a journal entry, reflecting in silence or enjoying God's creation by going for a walk. For many of us, worshipping with music and song is an important part of drawing near to God and will be a regular feature of how we connect to God in intimate worship.

William Law in his spiritual classic, *A Serious Call to a Devout and Holy Life*, says the following about singing our psalms of worship to the Lord:

> Just as singing is a natural effect of joy in the heart so it has also a natural power of rendering the heart joyful . . . There is nothing that so clears a way for your prayers, nothing that so disperses dullness of heart, nothing that so purifies the soul from poor and little passions, nothing that so opens heaven, or carries your heart so near it, as these songs of praise. They create a sense and delight in God, they awaken holy desires, they teach you how to ask, and they prevail with God to give. They kindle a holy flame, they turn your heart into an altar, your prayers into incense, and carry them as a sweet-smelling saviour to the throne of grace.[14]

It is so often in these intimate moments of worship, declaring our love for the Lord, that he cannot help but whisper back his love for us. At a conference, one of our ministry team leaders was praying for another lady as the song 'He Loves Us, Oh How He Loves Us' played in the background. As she was praying, the Holy Spirit began to impress so deeply on her the radical reality of that truth, that she stopped praying for the other person and declared aloud, 'He loves *me*! He loves *me*!' Worship is drawing near; a love response to a God of love. Worship is the interplay between songs of deep and sound doctrine and deep and sound longings for God, involving head and heart, mind and body, soul and spirit. Worship is the 'deep' of me longing for the 'deep' of him (Psalm 42:7).

Praise and worship inevitably end up in glory, be that the glory of right priorities, right choices, right perspective or eternal reward. They also invite encounters with the God of glory, who inhabits the praises of his people. Fire always falls on sacrifice, as worshippers in scripture so often discovered. A pursuit of God in praise and worship, with no other agenda than to glorify and enjoy him, leads us to the unexplored paths of his powerful presence and perfect peace.

We have discovered that when you prioritise God's presence you often get far more done by accident than on purpose because when the God of glory invades, transformation happens. In the presence of the Holy One, fears melt, courage grows, grace multiplies and passion explodes. Anything can happen when the glory of God invades our worship. My advice in such moments is to linger longer, learn to abide, wait upon the Lord and see what he will do. True refreshing for the deepest part of our being happens when we learn how to praise, worship and then stand in his glory.

UP
Connection

OUT
Calling

IN
Character &
Community

CHARACTER &
COMMUNITY (IN):
Ideas, Identity and Behaviour

# GOD'S BIG PICTURE:

## The gospel in four words

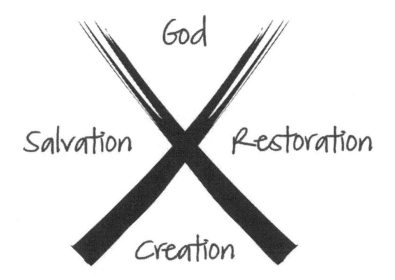

## understanding God's big picture (John 3:16)

God is working out history to his plan and we each have a part to play in the story that he is writing. **John 3:16** sums this up: 'For God so loved the world that he gave his only Son that whoever believes in him will not die but have eternal life.' This good news (the gospel) can be summed up in four words: God, Creation, Salvation and Restoration. This is the good news we are each privileged to demonstrate and pass on to those who don't yet know Jesus.

# God

'For God . . .' (John 3:16). The story starts and ends with the eternal God. There is only One God (Deuteronomy 6:4), who is revealed in the Bible as three persons: Father, Son and Spirit (Matthew 28:19; Ephesians 2:18). Yet each person is fully God. An amazing mystery and a profound reality!

**God the Father (Luke 15:11–32)** God is the Father of all creation, and part of Jesus' primary mission was to reveal what the Father is truly like. In his remarkable story about a wayward son, Jesus describes the Fatherhood of God. He is *generous, releasing, passionate, intimate, forgiving, engaged* and *unconditionally loving*. This is the Father you have been waiting for!

**God the Son (Revelation 1:12–18)** Jesus is God's son and in his life, death on a cross and resurrection he represents the Father perfectly (Hebrews 1:3). Revelation 1 gives us a glimpse of some of the characteristics of God the Son: Jesus is our *mediator,* the *Holy One,* the *Judge of heaven and earth*, our *strong deliverer*, the *King of all authority*, the *Word of God* and the *Eternal One*. Jesus has no rival. No wonder we join the angels in worshipping him!

**God the Spirit (John 14:15–27)** John 14 shows us seven different aspects of God the Spirit. He is our helper, the Spirit of Truth, God's presence, the Spirit of adoption, the revealer, teacher and the Spirit of supernatural peace.

# Creation

'. . . so loved the world . . .' (John 3:16). The universe and our world were made by God and he said that they were good.

Everything God creates reveals something of his beauty, goodness and power. He creates, sustains and nourishes all things by his words, because he cares for this planet! But creation has been spoilt by our decision to ignore, disobey and reject him. Sin separates us from a perfect God and creates the possibility of spending eternity separated from him forever (2 Thessalonians 1:9). Sin causes division, confusion, sickness and pain that affect all of our lives on this earth.

## Salvation

'. . . that he gave his one and only Son, that whoever believes in him shall not perish . . .' (John 3:16). God is the God of grace and mercy, so he sent his one and only Son into the world to die the death our sin deserves, in order that we could be rescued from evil, which is what 'salvation' means. Jesus, at the cross, paid the penalty for sin and by his resurrection gives us power to live a new life. Trusting in his death and resurrection causes us to be spiritually born again on the inside. We have been saved by God's grace and placed into his family called the church (Ephesians 2:1–10; 2 Corinthians 5:17–19; 1 Peter 2:9–10).

## Restoration

'. . . but have eternal life' (John 3:16). God is now restoring all things to his original plan, starting by bringing many people to know him in this life but also preparing a new heaven and new earth where they will live forever with him. This is a place where there is no more sickness, no more tears and no death. Jesus will one day come again to judge the living and the dead and gather to himself those who worship him. Until that day, the church is called to announce and demonstrate this good news, making disciples of all nations.

**Key Questions:**

How has being in a relationship with Jesus changed your life? What has God rescued you from, and what has he drawn you into? Spend some time being thankful.

Practise sharing the good news of Jesus (the gospel) with a friend. Ask them for feedback; did it make sense, is there anything you could change for next time?

Are you living a life full of the Holy Spirit? How are you making sure that your life is a Spirit-filled one?

**Additional Resources:**

Read and Use: *The Message of Jesus* booklet, www.kingsarms.org/messageofjesus

Watch/Listen: Tim Keller, *What is the Bible Really About,* http://vimeo.com/5428141

Read: Michael Reeves, *The Good God: Enjoying Father, Son and Spirit* (Paternoster, 2012)

Read: Jack Frost, *From Slavery to Sonship: Your Destiny Awaits You* (Destiny Image, 2006)

Listen: Terry Virgo, *Baptism in the Holy Spirit*, www.kingsarms.org/baptismterryvirgo

# View From the Front Line: Disciples in the Big Story of God

One Christmas, I purchased a 1,000-piece, pre-owned jigsaw puzzle depicting a beautiful Christmas wonderland. However, what began as an exciting endeavour in recreating the wonderland, slowly concluded in frustration as it dawned on us that, as with many second-hand jigsaws, there were pieces missing. Lesson learnt! The reality check was this: each piece of the jigsaw was vital, yet only found its meaning when connected to the bigger picture. The *micro* needs the *macro* and finds no meaning unless it is part of something bigger and more majestic than itself.

Ultimately, God is not part of our story; we are part of his. Disciples understand that we only truly find our purpose when we find it in God's. God is painting on an eternal canvas and each disciple is a beautiful brushstroke on the pages of his-story. Our lives have meaning because we are caught up into the breathtaking salvation plan of the God of grace. We are jigsaw pieces in God's majestic masterpiece, a cosmic story that weaves together our lives in his.

Our lives are not like a number in a phone directory, disconnected and unrelated to the numbers either side of it; rather, they are like lines in a grand narrative that God is writing, where each line builds on what has come before and prepares for what is coming later. God is building us together to become a dwelling in which he lives by his Spirit (Ephesians 2:22). God is working the end of the ages to a defined outcome where disciples from every tribe, people, nation and tongue will declare his praises in a new heaven and earth.

Knowing the big picture of *God, creation, salvation and restoration* is crucial for disciples, because context always supplies meaning. Years ago, when I was just a small boy, I greatly shocked my parents one day. Growing up as the son of a pastor, having always gone to church, I one day dropped the following bombshell: 'You two don't act much like Christians!' They immediately stopped me in the middle of the street, shocked at the words that had just tumbled out of their child's mouth. 'What do you mean "we don't act much like Christians"? What have we done wrong?' they asked, in tones of concern and disbelief. 'You know,' I said, 'U2, the rock band . . . they don't act much like Christians!' The relief on their faces was tangible and visceral. Context always supplies meaning.

Disciples only understand their meaning in the context of God's great story, which finds its zenith in the person and work of Jesus. In our self-infatuated world of entitlement and consumerism, disciples need more than ever to see the story God is telling, for this alone provides the true meaning we all seek and need. The Big Story is of the King and his kingdom. It begins with *God*, and moves through his *creation and salvation* to the final *restoration* of all things in a new heaven and earth.

Jesus himself understood the Big Story and sought to draw his disciples into the divine perspective he lived from, saying to them, 'But blessed are your eyes because they see, and your ears because they hear. For truly I tell you, many prophets and righteous people longed to see what you see but did not see it, and to hear what you hear but did not hear it' (Matthew 13:16–17).

It is in Jesus that the big picture of the kingdom is fully realised, because he is the long-awaited King. Through the Bible from Genesis to Revelation, the story that is being told is the story of King Jesus. Jesus understood the meaning of his life in the context of God's Big Kingdom Story.

God is the eternal King of Genesis 1. He has always existed and needs nothing outside himself. He is the perfect Three-in-One God, Father,

Son and Spirit. God is the creator King of Genesis 2, making all things for his glory and our pleasure. God is the rejected King of Genesis 3, spurned by the very beings he himself fashioned and breathed life into. From this point onwards, God is working out his plan of salvation and ultimate restoration, promising that one day the offspring of Adam and Eve would crush the head of Satan in ultimate victory over the sin sickness that would blight humanity (Genesis 3:15).

The Old Testament writings all pointed towards the coming King, who would reign again in perfect righteousness and grace, undoing the rejection of Eden and ushering in a new age of God's favour and mercy.

Later in the Old Testament, during Israel's darkest days, when the people's continuing rejection of God had resulted in war, famine and exile, and the light had almost gone out, the prophets heralded the hope that God's King would one day come back because God had not finished writing the Big Story of history. Indeed, God's intention was not merely to restore the fortunes of the one small nation of Israel, but to redeem the whole planet.

They spoke of a day when the King would personally visit the earth and bring the kingdom in its fullness. In that day the lame would walk, the blind would see, captives would be freed and new life would be poured out. Everything that had gone before was just a model of the greater reality of the kingdom to come.

The prophet Malachi ends the Old Testament with God's promise of a coming saviour: '"I will send my messenger, who will prepare the way before me. Then suddenly the Lord you are seeking will come to his temple; the messenger of the covenant, whom you desire, will come," says the Lord Almighty' (Malachi 3:1).

Hundreds of years later, as John the Baptist saw Jesus approaching him at the river Jordan, he declared, 'Look, the Lamb of God, who takes away the sin of the world! . . . I have seen and I testify that this is God's Chosen One' (John 1:29,34). The King of Eden had returned as the King of the Cosmos and did so in the most unlikely way, as a poor preacher from the northern backwater town of Nazareth, part of an occupied nation, suppressed and subdued. Yet in Jesus the unexpected happened. Eternal salvation entered the Big Story, not through the force of arms or overthrow of human will, but in a manner most unlikely of all – a wooden cross.

Contrary to all human logic and reason, the wisdom of God is revealed in the humility and grace of Jesus. The King shows his glory in sacrifice, substitution and selfless love; the King crucified then resurrected for us. Jesus saw the whole jigsaw and knew his place in the centre of the unfolding story of creation. He was the offspring of Adam and Eve, crushing the head of Satan, redeeming mankind with his own blood and purchasing men and woman for God (Revelation 5:9).

Salvation comes through the Son and through the Son alone. The creator King has come back in Christ or, as the Apostle Paul puts it, 'All of God's promises have been fulfilled in Christ with a resounding "Yes!"' (2 Corinthians 1:20 NLT).

Because we are partners and not pawns, Jesus enlists us in the family business of re-telling this Big Story and extending the kingdom. Our commission is to proclaim the good news of the kingdom to all creation, be that to individuals, families, neighbourhoods, cities or nations. The Big Story that the King has come back should impact all of life, in all of society, in every culture, everywhere.

One day, the story will conclude when the King returns in glory to finally usher in his perfected and permanent kingdom, where there will be no more pain, sorrow, weeping or injustice. A multi-racial, multicultural family will gather around the throne of God in new community – male and female, Arab and Jew, black and white – and we will sing together of the great eternal story, woven from Genesis to Revelation. It will tell of the creator God, who so loved the world that he sent his Son that we might become 'the ransomed of the LORD' (Isaiah 35:10 KJV), highly favoured sons and daughters of the Most High God, small but significant jigsaw pieces on the canvas of God's magnificent grace. Your life has meaning; but only in the context of Jesus the King. He is the Big Story.

# SHIFT YOUR THINKING:

## Knowing who you are IN CHRIST

## Seeing who we are in Jesus Christ

Paul writes to the Christians in Rome saying: 'Don't copy the behaviour and customs of this world, but let God transform you into a new person by changing the way you think. Then you will learn to know God's will for you, which is good and pleasing and perfect' (Romans 12:2 NLT).

The moment we started to follow Jesus, we received a brand-new identity as his children. We are no longer sinners, but saints; no longer trapped in our old life of alienation from God, but brought into a brand-new connection with our Father through the work of Jesus at the cross. 'Saints' are traditionally thought of as super-spiritual, extra-holy, miracle-working Christian heroes, but in the New Testament, the term 'saints' describes all believers in Jesus. A 'saint' is simply someone who has a brand-new identity as a child of God; released from guilt and condemnation, no longer imprisoned by sin and shame, but free to live as God intends us to. We haven't done anything to earn or deserve this, but when we're baptised 'into Christ', everything Jesus is, and everything Jesus won for us when he died and rose again, is credited to us like a payment into a bank account. This is what the Bible means when it says that we are 'in Christ'.

This requires a massive shift in our thinking. Our behaviour flows from our beliefs about what *we* think is true. Now that we are *in Christ*, our thinking has to line up with what *he* says is true in his Word, so that our behaviour and lifestyle begin to match our new identity. As Bill Johnson says, 'I can't afford to have thoughts in my head about me, that are not in His. It's impossible to be consistently effective in fulfilling His purposes unless I am continually training my mind to think of myself according to what God says about me.'[15]

Changing our way of thinking, however, is not straightforward. Humans are creatures of habit, and old habits do, literally, die hard! Recent research suggests that it takes approximately 66 days to form a new habit or way of thinking, as we replace old thoughts with new ones through constant repetition.[16] How do we achieve this change in terms of our Christian lives – and maintain it over time? Three things can help reinforce the truth of who I am in Christ: reading, reminding and remembering.

First, we feed our minds on what is true by reading the Bible and Christian books, and by listening to good teaching in church or online.

Second, we frequently remind ourselves and one another of the truth by speaking it out to ourselves, talking to others about it and asking others to encourage and remind us.

Third, we practise living out the truth daily in our thoughts, words and actions by remembering what is true.

Jesus said, 'You will know the truth, and the truth will set you free' (John 8:32). Freedom is an inside job: we shift our thinking with the truth of our new identity in Christ! The first two chapters of Ephesians draw out 6 remarkable '*in Christ*' identity truths for every disciple of Jesus.

### C: Chosen in Christ

'*Praise be to the God and Father of our Lord Jesus Christ, who has blessed us in the heavenly realms with every spiritual blessing in Christ. For he chose us in him before the creation of the world to be holy and blameless in his sight*' (Ephesians 1:3–4). We have been handpicked by the Father and brought into his family, blessed with every spiritual blessing. I am a chosen child, loved by the Father and adopted into his family forever.

### H: Handiwork of Christ

'*For we are God's handiwork, created in Christ Jesus to do good works, which God prepared in advance for us to do*' (Ephesians 2:10). We are God's masterpiece, his work of art and special treasure. Our lives have dignity, beauty and purpose because God fashioned us in his own image and glory.

**R: Redeemed in Christ**

*'In him we have redemption through his blood, the forgiveness of sins, in accordance with the riches of God's grace that he lavished on us'* (Ephesians 1:7–8). Every sin has been wiped away in Christ and his blood covers every sin carried out by me or against me. He redeems every part of my life and makes it brand new.

**I: Inheritance in Christ**

*'When you believed, you were marked in him with a seal, the promised Holy Spirit, who is a deposit guaranteeing our inheritance until the redemption of those who are God's possession – to the praise of his glory'* (Ephesians 1:13–14). I have an eternal inheritance that cannot spoil, fade or perish. Everything I do for Jesus is valuable and meaningful because my reward is in the hand of my God and is being stored up for me to enjoy in eternity.

**S: Seated with Christ**

*'And God raised us up with Christ and seated us with him in the heavenly realms in Christ Jesus, in order that in the coming ages he might show the incomparable riches of his grace, expressed in his kindness to us in Christ Jesus'* (Ephesians 2:6–7). I have been raised up to see things from God's perspective where Jesus rules as Prophet, Priest and King. I have become a citizen of a heavenly realm. I live knowing that I share in everything that belongs to Christ and am a partner with him in making the goodness and glory of God known on earth.

**T: Temple of the Spirit in Christ**

*'In him the whole building is joined together and rises to become a holy temple in the Lord. And in him you too are being built together to become a dwelling in which God lives by his Spirit'* (Ephesians 2:21–22).

God's presence lives and dwells in me and he has made me a perfect resting place for his Spirit. I am not alone but have received the Spirit of adoption and of power in Christ.

**Key Questions:**

How do you need to shift your thinking so that it is in line with who God says you now are in Christ? Where do you need to grow in your identity?

Which aspect of your identity in Christ do you have most revelation about at the moment? How does it impact your everyday life?

**Additional Resources:**

Read: Jack Frost, *Spiritual Slavery to Spiritual Sonship* (Destiny Image Publishers, 2013)

Watch: Simon Holley, *Identity Transformed* https://www.kingsarms.org/resources/media/message/identity-transformed.html

Listen: Terry Virgo, *Behold, a New Creation!* http://www.terryvirgo.org/media/behold-a-new-creation/

# View From the Front Line: Disciples Who Know Their New Identity

In our beautiful but crazy world of competing identity narratives, knowing who you are in Christ has never been more critical. Disciples who follow Jesus have been moved out of old ways of thinking about themselves and into the new reality of being adopted as sons and daughters of a loving heavenly Father. Knowing who we are in Christ changes everything because behaviour always flows from belief.

An example of how this principle changes us was played out on a recent family summer vacation on the Spanish island of Mallorca. Having arrived at our hotel, we stowed our bags and got changed for some time around the pool. Relieved to be there, we all made our way down the marble stairs ready to relax after a busy season and enjoy a much-needed holiday that we had saved for and been anticipating for a long time. Suddenly I heard a blood-curdling scream from the steps below me that sounded very much like my wife. With a growing sense of dread, I hurried down the stairs to find Carole on the ground, clutching her left arm. She had slipped and fallen down the staircase and, as we would later discover, had badly broken her radial bone and sustained an impact injury to her wrist. It was not a good moment.

Albert Einstein is credited with having coined the phrase, 'Adversity introduces a man to himself,' and I tend to agree with the great scientist. In moments of pain, loss and disappointment, who we believe we are determines our response to the situation. As my wife and I went through the process of paramedics, ambulance ride, health insurance, X-rays, arm manipulations and pain medication, we learnt something about who we are in Christ. We are not victims but loved children of God, and such knowledge profoundly transforms us.

Carole says that she has never known such pain as at that moment. As she sat and waited to be seen by a doctor, the temptations to self-pity, anger and 'victim thinking' tugged at her heart (as they did mine!). A dark and cavernous invitation to think like a pauper loomed in her mind. But Carole made a courageous decision that transformed that moment. She remembered who she really is and started to thank God for his blessings in her life. She recalled every answered prayer she could think of, every Bible promise and truth about her identity. She began to go to war against the old identity of feeling abandoned, lost and alone. As she did so, the hospital corridor turned from a place of pain into a place of worship. Joy, peace and the presence of God filled her heart with powerful heavenly influence, washing through her heart and mind, bringing strength and grace for that moment. Knowing who you are in Christ gives you a different lens on the world.

Jesus' public ministry began from a place of victory in this very arena of identity. Standing in the baptismal tank of the river Jordan, Jesus heard the sweet and powerful declaration of his Father: 'You are my son, whom I love; with you I am well pleased' (Mark 1:11). Before any public miracle had taken place, Jesus received what he most needed, which was a reminder of his heavenly identity.

From this place, Jesus entered forty days of wilderness testing, where the common denominator in each temptation was the opening phrase 'If you are the Son of God . . .' (Luke 4:3,9). Even the enemy of our souls understands that if he can keep us from believing who we really are, he has already dented any potential kingdom impact we may have. The enemy attacks our identity again and again with a dizzying mixture of accusation, deception and false information. He really is the 'accuser of our brothers' (Revelation 12:10). Jesus shows us how to fight in such moments, responding with a simple 'It is written . . .' (Luke 4:4,8,12) to every identity test he undergoes. Jesus believed the very word of God that he himself had inspired and inhabited in his incarnate self. The very words he inspired were words that he now fought with.

It is this battle for the airwaves of the mind that is at the heart of transformation for the disciple of Jesus and unless we begin to define ourselves as God now defines us, the traps of performance, comparison, legalism, insecurity, fear and self-reliance too easily become the norm. Christianity is littered with these things because frequently we have failed to understand that salvation is not merely the removal of punishment (we don't get what we deserve) but the active bestowal of blessing (we get what we don't deserve). It is the difference between a gospel of mercy and the true gospel of grace.

You and I are now in Christ. What is true of him is now true of you. It sounds incredulous and scandalous to say such a thing, but that is the gospel of grace: God's Riches At Christ's Expense – G.R.A.C.E.! I no longer have the right to think or behave like a forgotten orphan or excluded pauper. I have died and risen with Christ. I am a new creation. I am an ambassador of the gospel. I have been given the very righteousness of Christ. I am forgiven, healed and set free. I am a living, walking dwelling-place of God's very presence, and everywhere I go, the kingdom follows. I am an empowered son or daughter who serves in love, because who I am is bound up with who Christ is, for me and in me.

As disciples who follow Jesus, we must do as Jesus did and fight for the truth of our redeemed identities, which have nothing to do with our performance but everything to do with God's grace, as set out in his Word. I am no longer a sinner but a saint. I am now in Christ and this changes everything, forever!

# EJECT AND WALK FREE:

Refer your life-defining moments to God

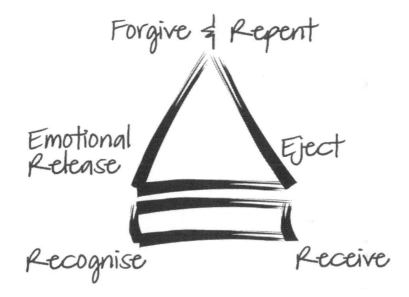

Forgive & Repent

Emotional Release

Eject

Recognise

Receive

Bringing lasting change through life's key moments

We are all shaped by the experiences and circumstances of life, both painful and positive. All of us will face disappointments and heartaches at some point in our lives and how we decide to deal with these is critical to our spiritual health.

Jesus spelt this out when he said, 'In this world you will have trouble. But take heart! I have overcome the world' (John 16:33). We cannot avoid every challenge, but we do have a God who can turn our battles into victories if we trust him and walk with him even through the tough stuff of life. He is the God of freedom who wants us to experience his power at work in our lives in a way that liberates us to help free others.

Ignoring painful experiences often seems like the easier option, but it cannot bring us into the deep freedom available for us through Jesus' power. We have to make the decision to walk towards God in pain, and not withdraw, because scripture promises that if we draw near to God, he will draw near to us (James 4:8). As we learn to bring these key life-defining moments to him, we experience the truth that Jesus promised, 'If the Son sets you free, you will be free indeed' (John 8:36).

A simple tool that helps us in this process of freedom is the framework of the acronym R.E.F.E.R. When we hit a life-defining event or situation that we need to respond to, we can walk through the following steps, which will help us renew our thinking and bring about transformation.

**R = RECOGNISE:** What does your response to this situation reveal about your beliefs? Are there any lies you've been believing about God, yourself or others? Can you recognise any patterns in the way you've responded to hurts, difficulties and disappointments in the past? If we habitually respond in a negative or ungodly way, it probably indicates that we're believing lies and we need to ask the Holy Spirit to show us if there is any part of the gospel that we are not living in the light of.

**E = EMOTIONAL RELEASE:** Express any emotion you may feel as a result of being hurt by other people. Express any disappointment you may have felt towards God or others. If you have been hurt by another person, imagine they are in the room and spend some time telling them openly and truthfully how their actions affected you and made you feel. Emotions are God-given and it's important for us to express emotion in the way modelled to us by Jesus and, in particular, the writers of the Psalms. The psalmists wrote incredibly honest and heart-felt descriptions of a wide range of emotions they experienced in response to all sorts of difficult circumstances. Jesus, too, experienced and expressed deep emotions such as grief and anger.

**F = FORGIVE AND REPENT:** Ask God to show you anything you've said or done that you need to repent of; it's important that we take responsibility for our own contribution to a difficult situation. Repentance means not only that we say we're sorry and ask for forgiveness – it also means that we turn away from that attitude or behaviour and resolve not to respond in that way again. You may also need to ask God to show you anybody you need to forgive. In both cases, be specific about what you're forgiving someone for, or what you're asking God to forgive you for (Luke 6:37; Matthew 6:15).

**E = EJECT:** Eject from your life any lies you've been believing and living under. First, declare out loud, 'I break agreement with the lie that says . . .' Then ask the Holy Spirit to show you the truth in place of the lie. Speak the truth out loud to displace the lie. It may sound strange to speak thoughts and ideas out loud, but in fact it's a powerful way of changing our mind-set.

**R = RECEIVE:** Expect the Holy Spirit to fill you with his power and joy and love. Spend time praying blessing on anyone who has hurt you. In the days following, spend time focusing on the truth by connecting with God in his Word and in prayer.

**Key Questions:**

How are you doing at embracing a life of authenticity and openness?

Who in the church really knows you?

Is there anything holding you back from being all God has called you to be and doing all that God has called you to do? You might find it helpful to book some time with a friend to pray these things through.

**Additional Resources:**

Read: Simon Holley, *Sustainable Power* (Authentic Media, 2013)

# View From the Front Line: Disciples Who Walk in Freedom

If ever there was a biblical story that portrayed freedom, it is the story of the prodigal son in Luke 15. You might find it helpful to stop and read it before reading the rest of this chapter. Jesus tells this parable in response to religious leaders who were scandalised at him spending so much time with tax collectors, prostitutes and sinners. He responds to their offence by telling them the story of a young man we now know as 'the prodigal son'. The word *prodigal* literally means wasteful. Jesus' message is clear: 'I came for the broken, the bruised, the lost and the oppressed. I came for the ones who have wasted themselves on cheap, worthless imitations of the Father's love. He has sent me to recover the wasteful ones.'

As we read the story Jesus tells, we discover the wasteful son finding his freedom in a life-defining moment. Such moments are known as *kairos* moments from the Greek word *kairos*, which means an occasion of special significance; in Christian terms, an opportune moment for God's divine favour to bring about breakthrough in our lives, if we will learn to refer it to him in the process. Our greatest challenges are so often the canvas on which God chooses to create his best artistry. The prodigal son could never have experienced the revelation of grace, had he not first come to grips with his own pride and pain.

Typically, our culture and upbringing teach us to suppress, bury or ignore our feelings of frustration, pain and disappointment in the deep, locked vaults of our subconscious. There they lie, buried but not dormant. Unprocessed pain has a habit of sneaking up on us when we least expect it or want it, often with damaging and even devastating consequences. Human beings were designed to walk with God, not away from him, through the pains of life, as he alone can unravel the mysteries of the heart and bring us to a place of freedom and peace.

As the prodigal son discovered, processing pain constructively, under the guidance of the Holy Spirit, can lead us back into an experience of healing in the Father's arms.

I'll never forget sitting in my friend Simon's office shortly after moving to Bedford, UK. The route to arriving there had not been straightforward but fraught with complexity, disappointment and a large measure of pain, none of which I had processed at all. I had adopted the typically British 'stiff-upper lip' approach to resolving heart issues, which as far as I'm aware has never helped anyone, ever. I didn't know it at the time, but as Simon asked me how I was feeling about it all, I was about to refer a life-defining moment to God and find significant freedom. Like the prodigal son, it was my moment to meet the Father again.

The first step in freedom is to *recognise* there is an issue to sort out. This is not always as straightforward as it might sound! As Simon asked me how I was feeling, I lied and said I was fine, though in reality I was hurting and angry but didn't quite know how to express it. As he probed a little deeper, I mentioned that I was struggling a bit, so he suggested we pray and bring it to God there and then. As we invited the Holy Spirit to fill the room and my heart, I started to connect with how I really felt. I recognised that not all was well in my soul. I saw my need for freedom. Like the prodigal son I, too, had a moment when I 'came to my senses' (see Luke 15:17). My journey to freedom, like his, started with the recognition, 'This hurts, and something has to change.'

Recognition often brings with it *emotional release* as we start being truly honest with God and ourselves. Emotions are not evil; emotion is a gift from God, who is himself emotional, in the holiest, healthiest and purest sense of the word. Our God grieves, mourns, laughs and celebrates. Emotional connection is a crucial part of healthy, whole humanity, enabling us to love and care for others deeply, just as God does for us. As I recognised that not all was well in my soul, Simon asked me to begin expressing, to those who had hurt me, how they had made me feel. This felt strange, because those people were not in the room at the time, so rather self-consciously I started to speak out loud my anger and pain. To my great surprise, what had started as a mainly cerebral process quickly transferred to an emotional one, as my feelings caught up with the words coming out of my mouth. I can tell you now, it wasn't pretty or quiet! Tears flowed and emotion gushed as the build-up of frustration and angst poured out in a torrent of truth and confession.

The prodigal son, too, went through this moment of emotional connection to his pain. The route back to the father was first through understanding the deep sorrow and pain of his own actions. 'I will set out and go back to my father and say to him: "Father, I have sinned against heaven and against you. I am no longer worthy to be called your son; make me like one of your hired servants." So he got up and went to his father' (Luke 15:18–20).

Emotional release is critical to being a healed, free disciple. It is very difficult to forgive from the heart if we cannot first get to the heart of the pain. We must learn to process well with the Father, speak out what hurts, address what needs mending and allow God to rush in where we need him the most. As I sat there crying, I also knew that I was starting to heal in that very same moment.

Once my words began to dry up and I had expressed every last ounce of pain, Simon led me through the process of *forgive and repent*. Just as I had spoken out loud my anger, he now asked me to do the same with forgiveness. To my surprise, my heart already felt softer, more compassionate, more able to extend mercy. Where before I had wanted blood, now I wanted reconciliation. It's incredible what the Holy Spirit does in our hearts in those moments – it is truly miraculous!

I also began to repent of my own wrong-doings. It is extraordinary how pain can become a mask that hides our own failed responsibilities or neglect. As Elton John famously put it, sorry seems to be the hardest word for so many people.

Again, the prodigal son mirrors this very same process. Returning to the father, he begins to make restitution for his wrongs. He confesses his wastefulness, his need and his longing to come back home. Almost in the same moment, the son walks through the crucial step of *ejecting* his past and committing to his new future. The Bible simply says, 'So he got up and went to his father' (Luke 15:20), which sounds simple enough until we realise that he would have to walk through the very villages and towns where people knew the scandalous thing he had done. In first-century Middle Eastern culture, the son's shameful dishonour of the father was punishable by death. Repentance for the prodigal son involved more than words. It involved a complete ejection of his former life, with whatever consequences might follow.

The love the prodigal son *receives* from the Father on his return home is the last and most joyous piece in the freedom process for the disciple. 'But while he was still a long way off, his father saw him and was filled with compassion for him; he ran to his son, threw his arms round him and kissed him . . . "Quick! Bring the best robe and put it on him. Put a ring on his finger and sandals on his feet. Bring the fattened calf and kill it. Let's have a feast and celebrate"' (Luke 15:20–23). The prodigal traded pigs' food for the father's love. His world was forever changed by an encounter with grace, which brought lasting freedom.

As I discovered that day, walking through the processing of referring my *kairos* moment to God, led to an encounter with the Father's love which was both beautiful and glorious. I was free.

This simple discipleship tool has brought freedom to countless people through the years as we have prayed them through the five simple steps of referring life-defining moments to God. And once we are free, we can help others to find the same freedom: 'Free people free people.' The goal is always to bring people home to the Father's love, where true freedom is always found.

'The love of God is the answer to all the "whys" in the Bible: the why of Creation, the why of the Incarnation, the why of Redemption . . . If the written word of the Bible could be changed into a spoken word and become one single voice, this voice, more powerful than the roaring of the sea, would cry out: "The Father loves you!"'[17]

# RECHARGE:

Recharging your batteries and living a healthy life

Spirit
Relationships
Mind
Emotions
Body

Living a healthy life in body, mind, spirit, emotion and relationships

God created the first man and woman. He created them to live a healthy and fruitful life in body, mind, spirit, emotion and relationships (Genesis 1:27–28). Their source of life was God himself. The entry of sin and the presence of evil in the world has brought with it difficulty and pain in each of these five areas that make up our humanity. The good news is that Jesus entered human history to give us life and life in all its fullness (John 10:10).

Jesus enables and empowers us to live the healthy and fruitful life God intended, as we walk with him and help one another. Jesus' goal is that we learn to love him with all our heart, mind, soul and strength and to love our neighbour as ourselves (Luke 10:27).

To live a healthy life, we need to be aware of how we are doing in each of the five areas, and how to recharge the ones that are running on empty. Using this tool, we can assess how we are doing and, where necessary, take action to recharge those batteries!

**Spirit:** 'Only take care, and keep your soul diligently' (Deuteronomy 4:9 ESV). How full or empty is your spiritual battery? How is your walk with God, your prayer life, Bible reading, worship and hearing God? What depletes you spiritually and what do you need to stay spiritually full?

**Relationships:** 'By this everyone will know that you are my disciples, if you love one another' (John 13:35). How are the key relationships in your life: spouse, family, children, parents, friends, co-workers? Where are relationships strained and where are they thriving? Is there anyone you need to forgive? Anyone you need to challenge? How are your boundaries in those relationships; too tight or too lax?

**Mind:** 'Whatever is true, whatever is honourable . . . whatever is pure, whatever is lovely . . . think about these things' (Philippians 4:8 ESV).

How full is your mental battery? How is your mental health, your thought life, your beliefs about God and yourself? How do you learn? Are you learning at the moment? What depletes you mentally and what do you need to stay mentally full? Are you glorifying God with your mind?

**Emotions:** 'For the kingdom of God is not a matter of eating and drinking, but of righteousness, peace and joy in the Holy Spirit' (Romans 14:17). How full is your emotional battery? How is your emotional health, your internal joy, sense of expectation and peace? Do you know and feel you are loved? What depletes your emotional battery and what do you need to stay emotionally full?

**Body:** 'After all, no one ever hated their own body, but they feed and care for their body, just as Christ does the church' (Ephesians 5:29). How full or empty is your physical battery? How is your sleep, exercise, diet, health? What depletes you physically and what do you need to stay physically full? Are you glorifying God with your body?

---

**Key Questions:**

Which part of your battery feels most healthy at the moment? Why?

How does your battery get depleted and recharged in the five different areas?

Which part of your battery needs recharging?

---

**Additional Resources:**

Read: Gordon MacDonald, *A Resilient Life* (Thomas Nelson Publishing, 2005)

Listen: Phil Wilthew, *Rest as a Weapon*, kingsarms.org/restasaweapon

Listen: Simon Holley, *Handling Anger and Handling Emotions*, kingsarms.org/emotions

Use: Paul Johnson, *Staying Healthy Survey*, kingsarms.org/stayinghealthy

# View From the Front Line: Healthy Disciples

I will never forget the moment when my lack of spiritual and emotional health finally caught up with me. I was attending a New Year training week for students who had given up a year to serve churches up and down the United Kingdom. It was a week I had been to, spoken at and participated in many times before, but this year was noticeably different in one respect: all was not well with my soul.

I was rather relieved that I had no particular responsibility at the event that year, other than to look after my children and support my wife, who was one of the leaders. I had been working for a church in pastoral and prophetic ministry for several years but, for whatever reason, I was not running on a full set of internal batteries. I felt tired, lacking joy and demotivated; a fact which came home to me when my wife asked if I would like to come along to one of the meetings the next day and lead some prophetic ministry with the students. I immediately heard my inner but audible thoughts saying, 'No way – I just can't be bothered!' That single sentence sent a shock wave through my system as I suddenly awoke to the realisation that something was broken on the inside. My batteries were stone cold flat.

That moment was actually a vital turning point, as I began to ask the Holy Spirit and close friends what had gone wrong. The reality is that every human being is a complex web of interlocking spiritual, relational, physical, mental and emotional cogs that make up a healthy, whole individual. Being human is a complicated business and it can be intensely difficult to separate out the constituent pieces and work out exactly what needs fixing. Everything is connected to everything else, as the fields of medical, psychological and social sciences have told us for so long. Physical health can greatly impact mental health, relationships can greatly affect our emotions, and so on. We are complex people made by an intricate and brilliant creator, who cares that we live healthy, full and free lives.

My steps to recovery involved looking at each of my five 'batteries' and working out what needed to happen to bring refreshing and wholeness. I discovered, as many do, that I had become emotionally and mentally exhausted because of spiritual issues. The road to health started by understanding what had drained that battery and how I could recharge it again. It took a year's investment of time, honesty, prayer, rest and repentance to get back to a place of thriving, not just surviving. It was a humbling but ultimately re-energising experience.

Jesus was the model of a perfectly whole human being and he invested all the capital at his disposal to bring about greatest possible impact around him. He launched his public ministry with spiritual investment, because he understood that change happens from the inside out. Immediately after his baptism in the Jordan River, he entered forty days of solitude, sacrifice and delayed gratification as he overcame temptation and fellowshipped with the Spirit. As he emerged from this time, Luke records that he returned to Galilee in the power of the Holy Spirit and news about him began to spread through the whole countryside (Luke 4:14). Rather than starting with gathering finance for a ministry programme, he learnt what it was to operate from an overflowing spiritual battery.

Jesus then began to demonstrate the same care and attention to other areas of his humanity, moving on to build a healthy core of close friends and deploy them in the actual physical business of bringing the kingdom. Jesus' instructions to them included how to look after themselves on the journey, how to trust the Father for daily provisions and how to use the gifts God has given. They discovered their mental and emotional batteries being charged as Jesus slowly but surely unveiled the meaning of hidden parables and teaching, and as they shared the joy of sicknesses departing and freedom coming. Jesus paid close attention to every aspect of his and his disciples' humanity, taking them on the journey of spiritual, relational, physical, mental and emotional health.

Jesus demonstrates two things in this process. First, that there is an order to creating disciples who change the world. It begins with growing spiritual capital that can only be developed as we walk with the Lord through the highs and lows of life. Dependence on God and a lifestyle of worship will grow something in us that is of greater worth than gold. The world simply cannot afford disciples who run on empty. Nations change because of disciples who keep the spiritual fires burning. Sin is often a manifestation of spiritual fire that has been unattended to, because lack of joy in God inevitably leads to lesser things seeming more attractive than they actually are. Secondly, Jesus demonstrates that humanity is complex and we must pay attention to our holistic nature. If I neglect to look after my body, my ability to do all he has called me to may suffer. If I fail to keep growing and learning, my mind can easily become dull to the new adventures of influence he calls me to enter into. It all matters to God!

In truth, we ignore emotional, physical and spiritual red flags at our peril. Many have shipwrecked their future in God simply through forgetting to do the simple things well. God does not just give revelation *to* us, but *through* us. Our very personhood is designed by God to demonstrate spiritual truths, all of which lean us into a humble dependence upon him and each other. As the apostle Paul spells out, God's power is made perfect in our weakness (2 Corinthians 12:9). I need to rest. I need to pray, I need to hear God's word. I need deep friendships. I need to be known. I need space to think. I need physical exercise. I need to learn.

We have an impressive inbuilt capacity for connection, creativity and productivity, but only if we learn the natural God-given rhythms of grace. My life is a marathon, not a sprint, so I need to stay healthy for the long haul. No athlete trains to pull a hamstring and take themselves out of the race; rather, they train with care to stay in the race and cross the finishing line. The same is true of the Christian life: our goal is to finish the race marked out for us by God himself.

Do whatever you have to do to stay healthy because the best gift you can give to others around you is a healthy, fully energised and tanked-up self that is in it for the long haul. Do the simple things well, and your life will become a living message of the glory of God. Healthy disciples change the world.

# PAUSE AND REPENT:

Seeing change through Kairos moments

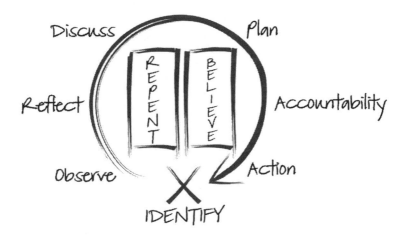

Learning and changing in partnership with God

At the very beginning of Jesus' ministry, he announces, 'The time has come . . . The kingdom of God has come near. Repent and believe the good news!' (Mark 1:15). Jesus has brought the kingdom of heaven to earth, and the process by which we participate in all that God has already won for us is to repent and believe. *Repent* simply means to change the way we think and instead believe a different set of truths.

Being a disciple means learning how to listen to God and learn from what he is telling us.

To help us with this, we can use a learning tool called 'Pause and Reflect'. This tool helps us recognise times when God is speaking to us through a moment of particular significance. The word *kairos* in the original Greek of the Bible means an occasion or season that is significant in some way. These key moments often provide the opportunity to engage with God and bring about change in our thinking, so that we begin to line up with heaven's value system.

It is vital that we take time to pause and reflect on what God is teaching us in these seasons of life so that we don't end up repeating our mistakes or missing God's blessings. Disciples are learners – they grow by bringing their *kairos* moments to God.

Using this tool, we move from observation to action in the process of repentance and belief. Working through the following steps when you hit a *kairos* moment in your life will enable you to learn to think differently as you partner with God's work in your life.

### Step One: Identify Your *Kairos* Moment

Thinking differently begins by identifying what *kairos* moment God is using in your life in this current season. *Kairos* moments are timely events, either positive or negative, that provide an opportunity for God to bring change in our lives. These could be key prophetic words we have recently received, a new revelation from scripture, a life-defining event such as bereavement  or marriage, or even a conversation that has left its mark in some significant way. They could be personal mistakes or successes. What significant moments is God using in this season to shape you? Identify these and then move on to step two.

**Step Two: Repent**

In step two we pause to work through the process of repentance, which involves taking stock and learning to think differently. Repentance is a deliberate decision to engage with what God is doing, reflect on how we need to think differently and begin to include others in the process. Work through the following three steps of repentance:

1. Observe: Change begins through observation. How have I reacted and responded to the *kairos* moment in question? How has it affected me emotionally, relationally and mentally?

2. Reflect: Take time to reflect why this event has affected you in the way that it has. Ask yourself: Why did I react the way I did? Why am I thinking the way I am? What is really going on under the surface? What are the roots in my beliefs that need adjusting? The more honest you are the better!

3. Discuss: Change is a community business. We change in the context of family. Begin to discuss your observations with trusted friends. Authenticity is a powerful weapon in leading us into freedom.

**Step Three: Believe**

Walk through the process of making and acting on a plan for transformation in your thinking. Adopt new beliefs that will bring lasting change.

1. Plan: What might God be calling you to do differently as a result of what you have learnt? Are there changes in behaviour, priorities or thinking that you might need to make? Be prayerful, asking the Holy

Spirit to help you put Christ and his kingdom first, so that your life can reflect the Father to those around you.

2. Accountability: Just as we need community in pain, we also need it in planning. Find at least one other person who you can share your plan with, who will help keep you accountable and on track with your decisions.

3. Action: Real faith always surfaces as action. Start living differently as a result of what God has shown you. Start now and keep going!

**Key Questions:**

How are you doing at learning from your *kairos* moments?

Which trusted friends in the church could you ask to help you pause and reflect on what God is saying to you?

In which areas of your life is God calling you to think differently? What effect will this have on your behaviour?

**Additional Resources:**

Read: Mike Breen and Steve Cockram, *Building a Discipleship Culture,* 2nd edition (3DM Publishing, 2014)

Explore: *The Imagine Network*, The Learning Circle https://imaginenetwork.squarespace.com/circle/

# View From the Front Line: Repentant Disciples

I used to believe that repentance was merely feeling sorry for something I had done wrong. I now understand that repentance, whilst sometimes including godly sorrow, is actually much bigger and more significant. Repentance is primarily about learning to think and believe differently so that we then behave differently. Disciples learn how to pause and repent so that they can think like Jesus.

The apostle Paul puts it this way: 'Do not conform to the pattern of this world, but be transformed by the renewing of your mind. Then you will be able to test and approve what God's will is – his good, pleasing and perfect will' (Romans 12:2). Repentance means to get back to God's perspective on reality and is how we are transformed.

This process starts with identifying what needs to change in our thinking. A number of years ago I remember praying and asking God to show me any offensive way in me, just as David did in Psalm 139:24. In all honesty, I was hoping nothing would show up on the repentance radar but, sure enough, God faithfully answered my prayer that day and said to me, 'You have an approval idol in your life and it's time to kill it!' The Holy Spirit had highlighted an issue I was not actually aware of up to that point, but it was a *kairos* moment in which he started a process of change within me.

As I started to walk the journey of repentance, armed with this new revelation, I began to reflect on all the moments in my life where I had made a decision based on earning other people's approval, rather than God's. There were more examples than I would like to admit and they all begged the question, 'Phil, why are you behaving like this? What is driving your need for other people's approval? What is the lie you are believing?' The answer was plain and simple: I was afraid of failure and rejection and needed people's approval to make me feel more secure about my own identity. The lie I was believing was that I was only valuable, safe or significant when others gave me affirmation, while the truth is that my value, security and significance are actually found first in God and my identity as his beloved son. It was a *eureka* moment. Because I had taken the time to pause and reflect, the moment became a key opportunity for change. It was time to think differently: to see myself from God's perspective.

The biggest war going on in most of our lives right now is the war between our ears. The Bible, when talking about this battle, says, 'For though we live in the world, we do not wage war as the world does. The weapons we fight with are not the weapons of the world. On the contrary, they have divine power to demolish strongholds. We demolish arguments and every pretension that sets itself up against the knowledge of God, and we take captive every thought to make it obedient to Christ' (2 Corinthians 10:3–5). Paul tells us that there is a fierce, ongoing fight in our minds in the realm of our arguments, pretensions, thoughts and knowledge; but that we need not be defeated, because God has given us divine weapons to demolish such 'stinking thinking'.

In order to eradicate a lie, you have to embrace a new truth – out with the old and in with the new. Once we have identified a lie, it must be isolated and starved while we introduce and feed a corresponding truth that lines up with God's word and perspective. Imagine for a moment that there is a dog in your back yard; a big, vicious dog that snarls and barks at you every day. Even though it is on a leash, you feel pretty darn scared of that dog but you still dutifully feed it, thus keeping it alive. Here is the secret: stop feeding the dog! When we stop feeding lies but start feeding a new truth, the old dies and the new forms. Very practically, this looks like memorising scripture, making positive declarations of what God says is true, and living in daily thankfulness and gratitude. Stop feeding the lies.

In my experience of pausing to repent, this process of renewing my mind started by reading books about my new identity in Christ. I also began to memorise most of Ephesians chapter 1, which speaks about the approval we have in Christ, and I would daily pray through this scripture as I spent time with the Lord. I made conscious decisions to say what I really thought in conversations with others, and when I felt tempted to be timid out of fear, I would remind myself of God's approval and my sonship. In daily decisions and small steps, I began to change and see things from God's perspective.

A crucial part of this journey was being open and authentic with others around me, because change is a community business done in fellowship and friendship. I began to share what God had said, the decisions I had made and even began to reference it in my public sermons. Accountability is not a dirty word, but a God-given means to help us achieve our heart's desires.

I have walked through this same 'pause and repent' process on many issues and I have discovered the kingdom advancing around me and inside of me every time, as I have learnt to think more like my heavenly Father. Jesus began his ministry with this call: 'Repent, for the kingdom of heaven has come near' (Matthew 4:17). He was announcing that it's time to change the way we think, because a new reality has arrived; the kingdom has come. Disciples take seriously the call to repent, because they know that the kingdom is at hand and want it to break out through them. The transformed mind is a powerful tool in the hands of God, so take time to regularly pause and repent and watch what God will do.

# HOME:

## Building a family through the 4Gs

Finding our purpose as part of a community
(Acts 2:42-47)

The church is not an organisation or a building but a family and the living home of the Spirit. The church is designed to be an inclusive and welcoming home for people from every tribe, language, nation and background (Ephesians 2:19–22). Jesus gave up his life for the church, loves it as his own bride and is utterly committed to building his family in a way that reflects his glory to the world (Ephesians 5:25; Matthew 16:18).

The early church is described in the following way in Acts 2:42–47:

> They devoted themselves to the apostles' teaching and to fellowship, to the breaking of bread and to prayer. Everyone was filled with awe at the many wonders and signs performed by the apostles. All the believers were together and had everything in common. They sold property and possessions to give to anyone who had need. Every day they continued to meet together in the temple courts. They broke bread in their homes and ate together with glad and sincere hearts, praising God and enjoying the favour of all the people. And the Lord added to their number daily those who were being saved.

What is clear from this scripture is that the church is not for consumers but for fully participating family members. None of us are spectators sitting on the sidelines, but each of us is called to get involved and play our part in family life! At The King's Arms, there are four major ways that we can get involved in making this church our home. We call these the 4Gs:

**GIVE:** *'They devoted themselves to the apostles' teaching . . . they gave . . .'* Every family takes commitment, and God's family is no different. Part of belonging is for each of us to GIVE commitment to our leaders, purpose, culture and financial needs. We are led by a team of elders (Titus 1:5–9) and many other leaders. Being part of the church means giving ourselves to follow

and **support our leaders** as they seek to serve the church. It means giving ourselves to live out the **purpose and culture** that we feel that God has called us to. Finally it means to regularly and cheerfully invest **financially** in the church by giving our money to meet the needs of our community.

**GROUPS:** *'. . . breaking bread in each other's homes . . .'* Participating in groups is the best way to build community and make friends in the church. It is also the best environment for ongoing and regular spiritual and emotional growth. At my home church, The King's Arms in Bedford, we have two types of small group. Missional Communities gather and support one another within a common mission based around particular people, places or passions. Lifegroups serve and support one another in following Jesus and reaching out in the place where God has already given them influence (work, school gate, etc.). Both types of group are places of connection, encouragement and adventure!

**GIFTING:** *'Teaching . . . praying . . . giving . . .'* God has equipped each of us with unique gifts and strengths. At The King's Arms we want to see every family member discovering, using and growing these gifts and serving God's vision through this local church. This is true whether our gift is hospitality, making friends, giving generously, prophecy, administration, playing an instrument, leadership or anything else. We naturally tend to serve in areas we feel confident and passionate about, but in the church, as in any family, we also look out for where there are needs and gaps where we can serve one another, whether or not it's our particular area of gifting and interest.

**GROWTH:** *'. . . the Lord added to their number daily . . .'* Our church exists for people far from God who do not yet know him, and we want to be people who invite others in our lives to experience the life-changing message of Jesus. Every healthy living thing grows, including the church! Playing our part includes inviting others who don't yet know Jesus to come and see what we have experienced of him and his church.

**Key Questions:**

Who could you invite to experience the church community?

What are your gifts, and which team could you join in the church to serve with them?

Are you financially giving regularly and cheerfully?

How do you feel about being led by others and coming under their care and leadership?

What type of group are you going to join, or is God calling you to start a new group?

**Additional Resources:**

If you are part of the family at The King's Arms and would like further information on how to get involved visit kingsarms.org/serving. Or to start giving visit kingsarms.org/giving.

For further information on current groups to join, visit kingsarms.org/groups. Alternatively, please investigate your own home church for ways to get involved more deeply.

# View From the Front Line: Disciples In Family

Discipleship cannot happen in a vacuum. As the famous African proverb reminds us, it takes a whole village to raise a child. In a world that is starving for genuine community, building churches that express genuine family, connectedness, relational strength and covenant loyalty is a big deal. No amount of social media and technology can replace the Christian disciple's need to find their fit in a church family and play their part in making disciples who make disciples.

My own growth as a disciple is intricately bound up with finding my home within a church community. I have been part of churches from before I was born, having grown up with a father who was a church leader. However, it wasn't until my early teenage years that I began to experience my own personal sense of belonging and buy in to my own church family. Three men had a huge impact on this area of my life, all of whom opened their homes and their lives to teenage lads like me and gave their time to encouraging, developing and calling out the best in us. My dear friend Jon commuted to a busy London finance job every day, getting home after 7pm every evening. He had a young family and a small flat in Brighton, yet every Tuesday he would faithfully welcome in eight lads to eat his food, mess up his home and do life together. I'll never forget some of those Bible studies and how formative the times of worship were in my life. I ate my first tiramisu with Jon, went shopping and talked about family life and shared car journeys where he challenged me about stepping up in my prophetic gift.

So often we find our purpose when we find our people, because our calling can only be worked out in deep connection with others. However, because true connection means covenant and commitment, many miss out on the joys of finding their home in a local church. Entitlement, fear of rejection and 'busyness' can all rob us of genuine belonging. We live in a culture that desires the benefits of intimacy without the sacrifice of covenant, but you cannot truly have one without the other; ultimately, we won't build anything great or worthwhile without giving our whole selves to it. Being a family involves sacrifice, buying in, participation. These are costly, but the rewards are great: the joy of laughter, loyalty, changed lives and a story to be proud of. The Bible simply does not conceive of a Christian who is not in covenant commitment to a local church family. Community can be messy, but doing life with people who are different from us is part of our message.

Four key signs of belonging – of being committed to the church family – are giving, groups, gifting and growth. Each of these activities represents a stance of the heart that says, 'This is not just your church, this is my church; these are not just your people, these are my people too.' The four Gs say, 'I belong here!'

**1. Giving**

Giving finance, time and energy is critical to a sense of belonging because, as Jesus pointed out, where your money is there your heart will be also (Matthew 6:21). Giving is a huge part of discovering joy in God because it really is more blessed to give than receive (Acts 20:35). R.G. LeTourneau was a hugely successful inventor of earth-moving machinery that forever changed how road construction took place and made him a multi-millionaire. His decision to live on 10 per cent of his income and give 90 per cent away is well known, but I love what he says about his experience of giving: 'I shovel money out, and God shovels it back – but God has a bigger shovel!' Giving is a privilege and a joyful adventure and is ultimately about our hearts, not sums of money. I want to give regularly, radically and cheerfully.

**2. Groups**

Being part of a small group is also critical to discipleship. I have been part of many groups that left an imprint on my life and enabled me to feel truly known, loved and inspired. I'll always remember, during my gap year in the States, being part of a group with two friends where we would ask each other awkward and honest questions in an atmosphere of complete acceptance. It changed me! I'll always remember running a small discipleship group for some older teenage guys in our church. We would pile round to McDonald's, Bible in one hand, Big Mac in the other, and talk about Jesus. Watching those guys grow in God remains one of the greatest privileges of my life. They have gone on to become successful architects, doctors, fathers, husbands and leaders and I am so proud of each of them. It changed me! I'll always remember being in a group whose mission was to love people in the town centre of Bedford, where I live. We would meet in town, pray together and then look for where the Holy Spirit was working and pray for the kingdom to show up. I often felt intimidated and nervous but, as I trusted God, I grew as a disciple. It changed me because that's what being in community does: changes you and calls you on in your walk with God. Christian TV can never do that for you – only community can.

### 3. Gifting

Discovering and using your gifting is also such a joy when you are doing life in a local church family. Typically, others can see gifts in you before you see them yourself, especially when they are still in embryonic form. We need others to call out the gold within us and give us an opportunity to serve. I remember once taking a team to lead prayer ministry at a youth event. Before the meeting began I challenged my team to believe God for some really specific words of knowledge that would unlock opportunities for breakthrough, and to ask God specifically for the names of people he wanted to bless. One lady, who had never tried anything so specific before, looked a little nervous but, in the context of community, was willing to give it a go, with us cheering her on!

As the time came for the team to bring their words, she stepped up and shared the names of two girls and God's word that he wanted to particularly bless their friendship and impact their school through them. In a room of a hundred teenagers, it turned out that these two girls were sat right next to one another, were best friends and went to the same school as each other! That night God particularly picked them out for a moment of encounter, because my friend had used and grown her gift through courage and obedience. I celebrated that evening because I'd seen a gift in my friend and had been able to watch it grow before my eyes. That's what happens in family. Community enables gifting to grow.

## 4. Growth

Lastly, we come to the area of growth. I recently pruned a tree in my garden so radically that I literally thought I had killed it. By the time I had finished, it looked like a dead stump of wood poking out of the ground, the most pathetic-looking tree you have ever seen. Yet within just a few weeks, green shoots were sprouting again because living things have a drive to keep growing! Commitment to a church family will automatically include a desire to contribute to the process of growth because that is what living things do. Disciples who belong want to extend that opportunity to others because we always recommend what we ourselves cherish the most. News this good just cannot be kept silent! Whether it is enabling growth in numbers coming to know Christ for the first time, growth of maturity or growth in influence within a locality, disciples are the essential growth engine of every church. To grow is to be alive.

Just as it takes a village to raise a child, it takes a church to raise disciples. Find your home and you will find your purpose.

UP
Connection

OUT
Calling

IN
Character &
Community

CALLING (OUT):

Ministry, Mission and
Multiplication

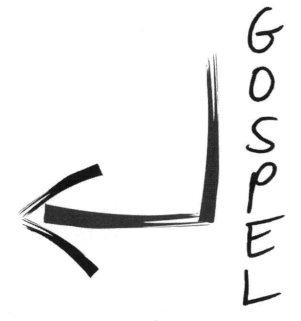

# ENTER THE ADVENTURE OF GOSPEL LIVING:

Returning to the good news every day

Six steps to sharing your faith

Moments before ascending into the heavens, Jesus commissioned his disciples to go into all the world and proclaim the gospel to all creation (Mark 16:15). The word gospel simply means good news – it is a report containing life-changing information for all who hear it and the message is this: Jesus is King and his kingdom has come! Through Jesus' life, death and resurrection we have the opportunity for hearts to be renewed, sins forgiven, consciences cleaned, guilt atoned for, shame removed and lives made brand new from the inside out. The gospel is the power of God for salvation and this news is something that every follower of Jesus is commissioned to carry wherever they go.

It's possible to live a busy and even fulfilling Christian life within the church without ever making a meaningful attempt to fulfil Christ's great commission. Sometimes words like 'evangelism' or 'mission' can scare us because they conjure up images of preachers screaming on street corners or doing things that put people off rather than love them well. Happily, living a gospel-shaped lifestyle is very different from these caricatures.

When Jesus sent his disciples to bring the good news, they discovered that it is one of the most joy-filled and life-giving privileges on planet earth. Not only did they get to bring the kingdom in a way that really helped and loved people, but they also got to be themselves whilst doing it. When the disciples returned to give Jesus the report of what had happened, scripture says that they were filled with joy (Luke 10:17). Joy was the natural by-product of sharing the gospel because there is nothing so beautiful as seeing people meet Jesus for the first time. It's what we were born to do.

The following tool, based around Jesus sending out the 72 disciples in Luke 10:1–9, helps us return to the good news and the adventure of gospel living. Live out the GOSPEL:

## G = God is on the move!

*Verse 1: 'After this the Lord appointed seventy-two others and sent them two by two ahead of him to every town and place where he was about to go.'*

God is on the move and we get the joy of joining in! The disciples were sent by Jesus to places where he was going to be. Sharing our faith and loving people is a beautiful and grace-filled privilege because we are working in partnership with God, going where he is going, knowing that he wants to do great things. Many of us can feel up-tight or inadequate when it comes to sharing our faith, but the gospel starts with knowing it is not about our performance but his goodness. The pressure is off – enjoy being on mission with God!

## O = Obedience is success

*Verses 2–3: 'He told them, "The harvest is plentiful, but the workers are few. Ask the Lord of the harvest, therefore, to send out workers into his harvest field. Go!"'*

Going is success! Jesus cares as much about our obedience as the outcome. Ultimately, only God can bring someone to himself, but we are partners with him in the family business; we are working with him in his harvest field. When you feel prompted by God to love someone, show kindness, share your God stories or bring the kingdom in some way, listen to his promptings, obey it and know that God is smiling – not measuring your performance, but delighting in your obedience. Then watch what he can do!

## S = Show courage

*Verses 3–4: 'Go! I am sending you out like lambs among wolves. Do not take a purse or bag or sandals; and do not greet anyone on the road.'*

Sharing the good news takes courage and God will sometimes deliberately put us in places where we feel like lambs among wolves, because we were born to trust him and see great breakthroughs in the midst of things that may intimidate us. Courage comes from knowing who God is and who we are in him. He is a good, faithful and powerful Father and you are his beloved child, with access to all of heaven's resources. Be courageous! Take courage to speak to others about Jesus, to love them the extra mile, to pray for sickness to leave and to bring words of knowledge that unlock kingdom power.

## P = Partner with people of peace

*Verses 5–6: 'When you enter a house, first say, "Peace to this house." If someone who promotes peace is there, your peace will rest on them; if not, it will return to you.'*

Jesus instructs us to look for 'people of peace'. Who are these people and how do we recognise them? Three things mark these people out. They are those who welcome you, listen to you and want to serve you. People of peace are those who are prepared to hear the message of the kingdom and whose hearts are open to you. People of peace will often show an interest in you and what you have to share, even to the point of serving, sharing or inviting you into their lives in some way. When you find these people, ask the Father how you can serve and communicate with them.

## E = Expect God's power and persevere

*Verses 8–9: 'When you enter a town and are welcomed, eat what is offered to you. Heal those there who are ill.'*

God's power flows wherever there is compassion and courage. Jesus considered it normal to eat in people's homes and to heal the sick at the same time! Loving people well includes believing God for miracles, signs and wonders and demonstrations of Holy Spirit power. Expect that God wants to speak to you and through you in prophetic ways that bless others. It's also vital not to give up – keep going, even if people are not immediately receptive. Love them, refuse to feel rejected and trust God for other doors to open.

## L = Lead people to Jesus

*Verse 9: 'Heal those there who are ill and tell them, "The kingdom of God has come near to you."'*

Ultimately, when the kingdom shows up, we have the beautiful privilege of introducing the king himself – Jesus. Our goal is that every person has the opportunity to start an authentic relationship with him. Very often, this process starts as we help people to come to God in prayer, ask for his forgiveness and invite him into their lives. Discipleship starts as a commitment to follow Jesus because it is all about him!

**Key Questions:**

How are you living out the great commission to proclaim the gospel?

Who are the people of peace in your life to invest in and serve with the good news?

How are you doing in loving others in both word and deed, and what step of courage might you need to take in sharing the gospel with others?

**Additional Resources:**

Read: Chris Kilby, *Equipped: Gearing Yourself Up for the Plans of God* (published by the author, 2017)

Watch: Simon Holley, *Jesus was Submitted to be Sent,* kingsarms.org/resources/media/message/jesus-was-submitted-to-be-sent.html

# View From the Front Line: Disciples Who Share the Good News

Fundamentally, we always tell other people about the things we love the most. Disciples of Jesus are those who share the good news of what Jesus has done not as a dutiful principle but as a delightful privilege. The power of communicating Jesus to those who do not yet know him cannot be underestimated. We have now become God's ambassadors and he is making his appeal through us, 'Be reconciled to God' (2 Corinthians 5:20). This is a high and beautiful calling.

My first forays into the world of sharing Jesus with others began in my teenage years with a growing sense of conviction that news this good could not be kept to myself. The great obstacle, however, was my own fear and sense of inadequacy for the task. Many of us don't lack conviction; we lack courage. Day after day I would walk into my Catholic school, thoughts nagging at my soul: 'Look at all these people who don't yet know Jesus, and most of them have no idea that I am even a Jesus follower!' It began to bother me more and more, to the point where I had to do something about it.

Praying about it one day, a genius strategy presented itself to me, though I would not necessarily recommend it today. I bought a hideous luminous green bag and some marker pens and proceeded to scrawl in large capital letters, 'JESUS LOVES YOU' and other such slogans. It wasn't pretty. However, as I plucked up the courage to walk into school the following day bearing the name of Jesus, something changed within me. For the first time, I found my courage and began to have conversations about my faith with my friends. One Taiwanese friend began to follow Jesus. Another came with me to a large gospel event to hear Billy Graham, and responded. One of my closest friends began attending my youth group and started to follow Jesus. Yet another came to church and came to Christ, followed by the rest of her family.

Suddenly, what had felt like a daunting and intimidating task became the most delightful and thrilling adventure of my life. I couldn't wait to see what God would do each day as people looked at my bag, often laughing but also asking genuine questions. For me, double science became less about protons and neutrons and more about Sophie and Siobhan who sat either side of me in class. Both were professing Satanists, complete with pentangle necklaces and gothic clothing, yet both were desperately hungry to talk about spiritual things, which we did every class. Eventually, I became so well known at school as a Jesus follower, that some of my teachers would ask me to close the lessons in prayer.

Sharing the good news changes lives, including our own! The gospel really is the power of God for the salvation of everyone who believes (Romans 1:16). When we talk about the one we love, God cannot help but back up the very message that he himself inspired and is the central hero in.

Thankfully, we don't all need to buy marker pens and green bags to share our faith. For me, it was an important beginning into the adventure of gospel living, but intentionally living and sharing the good news is meant to be a normal everyday part of our lives. It starts with understanding that God is already on the move. He is the great initiator and instigator of this rescue mission. We are willing participants in something that he himself is doing. All he requires is obedience and the courage to say yes. Ultimately, we are not responsible for the response of other people to our message. We merely need to posture our hearts to love God and love people well.

Nothing worth doing comes without a cost and often that cost is stepping through fear and into courage. We can feel like 'lambs among wolves', as Jesus so rightfully identified. This truth powerfully came home to my wife Carole one day when she popped over to talk to a neighbour about our excessively fruitful and rather overhanging pear tree, which had a nasty habit of depositing its contents perilously close to the neighbour's car. We were about to move house but wanted to leave on good terms and love our neighbours well by pruning the tree. Sharing good news starts by people knowing that we value them, irrespective of whether they respond to Jesus or not. We are called to love unconditionally and warmly. Ultimately, you only have as much influence in someone's life as they know that you truly value them. How we say things is as important as what we say because the messenger opens the doorway to the message.

As she stood chatting at the door, Jill, our neighbour, told Carole that she was in a great deal of leg pain due to an infection in her bones. She had been unable to sleep for weeks, was on strong medication and was in hospital regularly for tests. She was visibly in pain as she talked on the doorstep. Carole felt the Holy Spirit nudge her and knew she should offer to pray for healing for Jill, but she pushed the thought away, gave Jill the news about the tree and went home. But almost as soon as the front door closed behind her, Carole felt a conviction that she should go back and pray. The following day, making up an excuse to pop round again, Carole offered to pray for our neighbour. At the invitation, Jill looked left and right, as if to check no one was secretly watching, and pulled Carole into her house. After screaming at her kids to be quiet, Jill then rolled up her pyjama trouser to reveal the infected leg! Carole prayed a quick prayer asking Jesus to bring healing, all the while feeling Jill's eyes boring into her. There were no smells, bells or angelic visitations; it was normal, down to earth and over pretty quickly. Carole left the house, glad that she had obeyed but a little disappointed that nothing seemed to have changed.

A few days later, Carole knocked on Jill's door to find out if there had been any improvement. To her shock, Jill greeted her with a massive beaming smile, with her husband Gary and their two daughters alongside her. They explained that from the day Carole had prayed, Jill had begun to improve, to the point where she had been signed off by the doctor and was completely free of pain. It was like looking at a different family. They were open and grateful and, that day, the kingdom showed up because of simple, courageous obedience. Carole had found a woman of peace, open to the gospel, and God's power had shown up in a beautiful way.

People of peace are those who welcome you, listen to you and want to serve you. God is a relational God who loves to work through relationships of genuine connection and chemistry, so when you find these people, invest time, love them well and expect God's presence to show up.

And of course nothing can beat the thrill of actually leading someone to make his or her decision to follow Jesus for the very first time. These moments have been some of the best of my life. At the back of this book is a simple prayer, which is an easy way to help someone make a first-time commitment to follow Jesus. I was just 6 years old when I prayed a similar prayer in my parents' bedroom. It was undramatic yet entirely life-changing. My wife's experience was very different: she made her decision aged 16 when, as a member of a street gang, she found Jesus in a field. It was dramatic and also entirely life-changing. Quite how we step over the line into God's family does not matter, but the discipleship journey starts with this key decision and there is none more important in all of life.

## VOLUME DOWN:

Turning the volume down to understand your mission

Directional prophecy

Opportunities

Wants

Natural Gifts

Four questions to discern what God is saying to you and what you should do about it

Each one of us has a unique mission from God as part of his overall plan to fill the earth with the knowledge of his glory (Habakkuk 2:14; Matthew 28:19–20). Together we are called to bless and bear witness to Christ in all nations – 'in Jerusalem, and in all Judea and Samaria, and to the ends of the earth' (Acts 1:8). It is important that we take time to explore what God is saying to us, both personally and as a community, and think through how we should respond.

Whatever God says, it is always for the purposes of building the church, serving others and blessing the nations. In this way, we have the ongoing privilege of giving away the goodness of God to others, just as Jesus modelled! (See John 17:18; Luke 9:1–6; 2 Corinthians 5:20.)

Learning to tune into God's voice and turn down the volume of the other voices in our lives is vital to living a healthy Christian life. Different seasons of our life can bring different missions from God. The following four questions will help us discern the mission of God for us in the current season of life we are in, personally or as a community. We have to learn to turn the volume D.O.W.N:

**D = Directional prophecies:** What has God been saying? We are called to test the prophetic and hold onto what is good (1 Thessalonians 5:19–21) because it helps us to fight the battle well (1 Timothy 1:18). Jesus said that he would do nothing except what he saw the Father doing. Hearing his Father's voice was what directed and sustained his entire life (John 5:19). Using the Record tool, take time to consider what God has already said to you and what he is speaking today.

**O = Opportunities and needs:** What open doors do you or we have? God often guides us through the opportunities and invitations we have to serve him in each season. Joseph served in Pharaoh's court because he was given an open opportunity to rule (Genesis 41:39–40). Peter visited Cornelius' house because of a vision (Acts 10:1–23). Such opportunities are one of the ways God directs our path and we should take stock of the open doors that we have in our life (Colossians 4:5; Galatians 6:10; Ephesians 5:16).

**W = Wants:** What would you like to do? What do you enjoy doing? God uses our natural desires and passions to direct our serving. He loves to give us the desires of our heart (Psalm 37:4; Psalm 20:4). The apostle Paul longed to visit Rome so that he could preach the gospel there and impart some spiritual gift (Romans 1:10–11; Romans 15:23) which he eventually did, spending the last part of his life there. Our longings matter to God. Ask yourself what issues or areas of service naturally stir your heart and create a sense of excitement and passion. Have you noticed particular gaps or needs that you want to do something about?

**N = Natural Gifts:** What are your natural strengths and gifts? God uses our natural abilities to help us serve others with excellence. A strength is something you are both good at and enjoy doing (Romans 12:6; 1 Corinthians 12:1–11; Proverbs 18:16). It may be helpful to write down what you feel your gifts are. Additionally, you can ask those close to you what they feel you are gifted at. How could you serve others with these gifts and how might they build the church and bring the kingdom?

---

**Key Questions:**

What lies might hold you back from stepping into what God is calling you to?

What is the truth?

What action can you take in the next month to step into what you are called to?

---

**Additional Resources:**

Read: M. Buckingham and D. Clifton, *Now, Discover Your Strengths* (Pocket Books, 2005)

Read: Bill Johnson, *Dreaming With God* (Destiny Publishing, 2006)

## View From the Front Line: Disciples Who Know Their Mission in Life

I recently visited dear friends who lead a church in Wellington, New Zealand. During a team meeting, we were grappling with the question of what God was calling this particular church family into, both in the immediate present and further ahead in the future. These were disciples wanting to get a sense of clarity about their mission. It was at this point that we began to use the DOWN discipleship tool. Disciples of Jesus must learn to turn the volume down in order to get a proper God-perspective on their prophetic calling in life, whether as individuals or whole communities.

Isaiah 30:21 says, 'Whether you turn to the right or to the left, your ears will hear a voice behind you, saying, "This is the way; walk in it."' The truth is, we live in a world so beset with other voices, noises, cell phone alerts, Twitter notifications and Facebook feeds, that it can be difficult to hear the one voice that truly matters above all others. We are bombarded every day by a dizzying array of directions and demands. Turning the volume down is critical to hearing Jesus and his mission for our lives. Wayne Cordeiro says:

> When it comes to being heard by his children, our Father does not compete, nor does he contend for our undivided attention. Often he delivers nothing more than a nudge – easy to dismiss if you don't recognise the Source. He whispers, soft undertones that invite us to bend an ear . . . There is a frequency that your life was designed to be tuned to, and that frequency is the unique voice of God.[18]

In an age where we can be overwhelmed with options and opportunities, tuning into the right frequency takes deliberate time, attention and thought. God has a unique path for each of us, that we alone are called to walk in. As that team in Wellington began to turn the volume down, God's directions became increasingly clear. A clarity of mission emerged.

Directional prophecies are the first key part of discerning God's mission for your life or community. What has God actually said or prompted you to do? Years ago, as a teenager, I was working in the study of a well-known pastor and preacher. His walls were lined with thick commentaries and theological tomes and on his desk were various family photos and a small black index card box. Being a naturally inquisitive teenager who knew it was easier to get forgiveness than permission, I started to thumb my way through the cards in this mysterious black box. It was a box of promises. Every card had written on it a specific promise from God, either from scripture or a prophetic word that had been particularly significant. It suddenly struck me that behind the public visage of this man, who I respected, was a private devotion to living by the directional word of the Lord.

Becoming a good steward of the words God entrusts to us really is a big deal. So often, God's directional promises come to us in seed form to see whether we will nurture them or discard them. Will we care for, remember, pray through, cultivate and talk about the God-given dreams he has planted in our hearts? One way that I have tried to do that through the years, is to create a database of every significant word I have received from other people. A few years ago, God said to me that I needed to start living much more intentionally by the words he had given me, rather than by the demands and 'busyness' around me. In my mind's eye, I saw a picture of a 'promises wall' in my office, so I duly printed off every prophetic word I had received and stuck them to my wall. In the middle of them I wrote out 1 Timothy 1:18–19: 'I am giving you this command in keeping with the prophecies once made about you, so that by recalling them you may fight the battle well, holding on to faith and a good conscience.' Learning to steward directional prophecies is a great starting place for discovering your mission in life, but it is only part of the picture.

God guides us through the open doors and opportunities we find around us. Prophetic words have a timeliness to them that is often confirmed by circumstances in our lives. The apostle Paul had a clear directional prophecy about taking the good news of Jesus to non-Jewish people (Acts 9:15). In Acts 16 we find Paul and his companions attempting to bring the kingdom in the province of Asia, but the opportunity just did not seem to be there: the door was closed. During the night, Paul was woken from a dream, in which a mysterious messenger was inviting him to go to Macedonia instead. We read, 'After Paul had seen the vision, we got ready at once to leave for Macedonia, concluding that God had called us to preach the gospel to them' (Acts 16:10). Disciples learn to see God's guidance in both 'ordinary' circumstances and supernatural dreams and visions.

An equally powerful tool God uses to propel disciples into their mission is the passion and dreams we find within ourselves. Guidance can start with the simple question, 'What do you want to do?' As Jonathan and his armour bearer were contemplating attacking a Philistine outpost on their own, with no back-up, Jonathan began to find his direction in his own desires. 'Jonathan said to his young armour-bearer, "Come, let's go over to the outpost of those uncircumcised men. Perhaps the LORD will act on our behalf. Nothing can hinder the LORD from saving, whether by many or by few." "Do all that you have in mind," his armour-bearer said. "Go ahead; I am with you heart and soul"' (1 Samuel 14:6–7). Direction can come from the desires God places within us.

I remember sitting down with a friend who was contemplating God's call on his life. At the time, he was in a marketing job but felt a growing compassion and desire to work with the poor. 'What should I do? What is God saying?' would be the frequent topics of our conversations. Eventually I said, 'Well, what do you want to do? Do that and God won't be far behind!' Years later, he now leads a successful charity working with destitute asylum seekers, some of the poorest and most vulnerable people in our nation. The kingdom advanced because of his willingness to take seriously the God-given desires in his own heart. What is in your heart? Who do you long to reach with the good news? What people groups, tribes or neighbourhoods grip your heart when you pray? What do you long to see God do in the nation or in your next-door neighbour? These things matter, because God loves to use us in the things and people that we love.

Lastly, the natural gifts we carry can often give us a big clue as to how God wants to use us and in which ways. Sitting down with the team in Wellington, this was the last question we began to ask together. What has God given you by way of strengths, talents and abilities? How can you maximise your strengths and cover each other's weaknesses? What are you good at doing and how can you get better at that? The diversity and beauty of the gifts in the room was breathtaking to see as, one after another, the team began to call out the strengths they saw in their teammates. One had a brilliant natural ability to father and develop younger leaders, while another was brilliant at making friends cross-culturally with Maori-speakers. One was a gifted strategist while another was a pioneer and evangelist. As we went round the team, you could feel the guiding hand of the Holy Spirit confirming the mission of his disciples in that particular room.

Disciples of Jesus are committed to finding his mission for their lives, which we can only do when we take time to dial down the other noises of this life, to hear the one voice that carries the words of eternal life. What is God saying to you and what are you going to do about it?

# BRIGHTNESS UP:

## Turning up the brightness of the Kingdom

### Demonstrating the seven signs of the Kingdom in your sphere of influence (Isaiah 61:1-4)

> The Kingdom of God is God's reign in man's heart through Jesus Christ. This is the good news.[19]

We are called to demonstrate and declare the kingdom of God wherever we go, thereby introducing people to the reality that Jesus is alive and that God is good. The kingdom can simply be defined as the active rule and reign of God over all that he had made (Psalm 103:19; Daniel 4:3) and was the central message of Jesus and his disciples (Luke 4:43; Matthew 10:7; Acts 1:3). Mike Pilavachi says, 'The greatest evangelistic tool we have? Disciples. Men and women who look, sound and smell like Jesus.' Bringing the kingdom is living life like Jesus modelled. The kingdom of God reflects all that is true of its King, which is why Jesus taught us to pray, 'Father . . . your kingdom come, your will be done, on the earth as it is in heaven' (Matthew 6:9–10).

Isaiah 61:1–4 shows us seven key kingdom themes that we are called to demonstrate in our areas of influence:

1. We bring his **PRESENCE** into every situation: *'The Spirit of the Sovereign LORD is on me'.* You carry his presence to bring breakthrough into desperate places.

2. We bring his **JUSTICE** to the poorest and most marginalised in our culture, *'because the LORD has anointed me to proclaim good news to the poor'.* Wherever you find physical, emotional, financial or social injustice, God calls you to bring the kingdom.

3. We bring his **HEALING** to the sick and broken. *'He has sent me to bind up the brokenhearted'.* Sickness and disease and brokenness are called to bow to the name of Jesus. Lovingly, confidently pray for those who are suffering in this way.

4. We bring his **SALVATION AND DELIVERANCE** to those who don't yet know Jesus, *'to proclaim freedom for the captives and release from darkness for the prisoners'.* We carry life-changing news that brings eternal life to those who believe it and sets free those who receive it. Be bold in sharing!

5. We bring his **PEACE** wherever there is chaos, anxiety or distress, *'to proclaim the year of the LORD's favour . . .'* We carry favour from God himself, which releases heaven's peace.

6. We bring his **COMFORT** wherever there is suffering, *'. . . to comfort all who mourn'*. The comfort of God himself is the most sustaining reality.

7. We bring his **JOY** to all who mourn or despair, *'to bestow on them . . . the oil of joy instead of mourning, and a garment of praise instead of a spirit of despair'*. We have received a kingdom of joy, which has become our strength. Spread laughter and thankfulness wherever you go!

---

**Key Questions:**

Where are your areas of influence? (Who are your non-Christian friends? Where do you have contact with unbelievers?)

What aspects of the kingdom are bright in relation to your areas of influence?

What aspects of the kingdom would you like to turn up the brightness of?

Take a risk to see God's kingdom come in your area of influence over the next month.

**Additional Resources:**

Listen: to the series preached on 'The Kingdom of God', kingsarms.org/kingdom

Read: George Eldon Ladd, *The Gospel of the Kingdom* (Eerdmans, 1990)

Read: Derek Morphew, *The Kingdom: Healing the Dualism of Personal and Social Ethics* available at vineyardusa.org/library/the-kingdom-healing-the-dualism-of-personal-and-social-ethics/

# View From the Front Line: Disciples Who Carry the Kingdom

I live in the United Kingdom. I am a citizen under the rule and reign of Queen Elizabeth II and am one of her subjects. I live under its freedoms and am bound by its restrictions. Even when I travel outside my own country, I carry with me my UK passport which defines my citizenship, my identity, my belonging, my homeland. I am part of a kingdom and carry that wherever I go. Citizenship brings identity, access and purpose.

This is a limited yet powerful picture of what it looks like to be part of Jesus' heavenly kingdom. The biblical use of 'heaven' and 'the kingdom of heaven' has far less to do with geography than with domain. 'Heaven' speaks of the spiritual reality in which God rules, reigns and has dominion and, says the apostle Paul, all those who follow Jesus have now been made 'citizens of heaven'. (Philippians 3:20). I have dual citizenship in this world and the world to come. I have dual citizenship in the kingdom of this world and the kingdom of God. Just as my UK passport reminds me of my earthly sense of belonging, so God's Spirit and his Word remind me that I am now part of Jesus' kingdom. Wherever I go, I carry a heavenly kingdom with me and it is this kingdom that I am commissioned to extend to all the world (Matthew 24:14).

Nowhere in scripture is the kingdom of God explicitly explained or defined, yet it appears throughout, as one of the big stories weaving its way through every book. Jesus opened his public ministry with a call for his hearers to 'repent for the kingdom of heaven has come' (Matthew 4:17), and in his life, miracles, teaching, death and resurrection, the kingdom of heaven began to break into the here and now. This kingdom had been described by the prophet Isaiah many centuries earlier, when he predicted that a saviour would come from heaven, bringing with him a kingdom of peace, justice, comfort, healing, salvation and God's own presence and joy.

Now that we are in Christ, we, too, have the privilege of distributing the spoils of war won by the life and death of Jesus. We are agents and ambassadors of his heavenly kingdom, announcing to the world that the King has come and will one day come again to put every wrong right. Disciples of Jesus understand what they carry and are ready to give away the good news of the kingdom wherever they find themselves.

A friend in my church was walking along the street one day when a woman ahead of her, with two small children in tow, collapsed suddenly on the pavement. My friend rushed to help her, and the woman explained that she suffered from chronic fatigue syndrome and would regularly lose strength without warning. My friend, knowing herself to be a carrier of God's kingdom, offered to pray, and the woman accepted gratefully. As she prayed, God began to move so powerfully that the woman felt as if weights were lifting off her. Startled, she asked mid-prayer, 'What's happening to me?' Quick as a flash, inspired by the Holy Spirit, my friend replied, 'Well, sometimes when God pours in good things, bad things have to leave. That's what is happening to you right now.' Strengthened, revived and amazed, the woman was able to stand up and, as a result, opened her heart to Jesus right there in the street, where she had fallen just minutes earlier. That is the kingdom of heaven.

Our church started as an outreach project to the homeless in Bedford, and that river of God's compassion for the poor still runs deeply in us. Our work among the homeless has continued to grow year after year, as we truly believe that there is no such thing as a hopeless case. God can reach anyone, anywhere, irrespective of the barriers he finds.

Time and again we have seen the kingdom come most powerfully among the most vulnerable in our society. Our night shelter, an 18-bed hostel for rough sleepers, is currently led by a former resident, who himself was homeless just a few years ago but whose life has been transformed by Jesus. Another man was sleeping under a bridge in Bedford every night, feeling lost, alone and broken, with only his dog for company. No hostel would accept a resident with a pet until he came to our night shelter. Just a few years on, this former rough sleeper is now in his own accommodation with a steady job and a new church family. That is the kingdom of heaven.

Amju was visiting Bedford from her home country of India and had only one day before her return home. Although she had grown up a practising Buddhist, she had attended a Christian convent school and been impressed by the love shown to her by the nuns who ran the school. Being curious about the Christian faith, she wanted to visit a Christian church before going home, and decided to find a church by taking a bus and getting off as soon as she saw a church steeple. However, after half an hour waiting in vain for a bus, she stopped a passer-by to ask for directions. The passer-by was my friend Justin, who was on his way to our church service. Amju went with him and his two small children and arrived at our doors unsure what to expect. She quickly received a warm welcome and found a place to sit. During that particular service, our 8- to 10-year-olds helped to lead a time of prayer for those with sickness in their bodies. Calling out very clear and precise words of knowledge, detailing specific illnesses, one of the children shared a word that particularly struck Amju. 'There is a lady here; you own a pair of pink sparkly shoes and you have pain in one of your legs. Jesus wants to heal you this morning.' Amju responded to this word, was prayed for by the children and received instant alleviation of her leg pain, much to her delight.

As the talk ended and an appeal for salvation was given, Amju's hand was the first to shoot up as she accepted Jesus into her life for the first time. Tears of joy flowed because the kingdom had shown up in a most remarkable yet normal way. Whether you give a cup of coffee to a stranger, offer an invitation to church at a bus stop, pray for someone who is sick or lead someone to know Jesus, all are a beautiful part of bringing the kingdom. Wherever you go, the kingdom follows. Disciples understand that the things Jesus did, they are to do as well. It's time to bring the kingdom!

# MULTIPLY:

Multiplying disciples

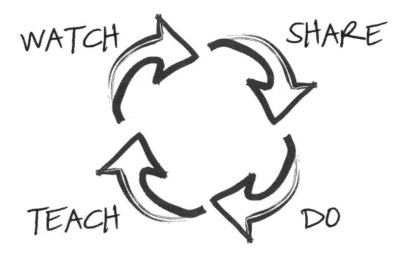

WATCH SHARE

TEACH DO

Releasing and empowering others into ministry

Jesus has called us to go and make disciples of all nations (Matthew 28:19–20). Discipleship is the intentional relational process through which we learn how to be like Jesus and do the things that Jesus did. Much of the time we learn new skills by imitating others and replicating what we have seen them do.

Both Jesus and the apostle Paul can be seen using these steps as they make disciple-making disciples (Luke 10:1–24; Matthew 28:19–20; 2 Timothy 2:1–2).

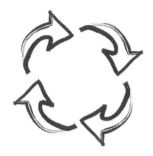

This process of imitation is vital if we are to effectively multiply disciples who can in turn multiply disciples.

The following four-step process helps us understand how to create a learning environment where we can release and empower others into works of ministry.

**Watch it**

First, take someone with you to observe how you do a particular task, asking them to actively watch and learn how you go about it. Discuss it with them afterwards, explaining what you did and why. Ask them for their own observations and answer any questions they may have.

**Share it**

Secondly, ask the person to join you and share in the delivery of the task itself, with you taking responsibility for preparing them well beforehand. Discuss together what you will do and how you will go about it and give encouragement and honest feedback after the event.

**Do it**

Thirdly, empower that individual to perform the task on their own, with you providing background coaching. Allow them to shape and direct the task without your intervention, as far as possible. Give them encouragement and feedback after the event.

**Teach it**

Lastly, release this individual to go and replicate this process with others and pass on what they have learned. As you watch them train others, celebrate that you have contributed to the mandate of Jesus to go and make disciples who make disciples!

---

**Key Questions:**

Who are you intentionally investing in?

Which of the four sections – Watch it, Share it, Do it or Teach it – do you find the easiest to do? Why?

Which section do you need to grow in? How are you going to put this into practice?

---

**Additional Resources:**

Read: Mike Breen, *Building a Discipling Culture* (3DM Publishing, 2011)

Read: Tony Stolzfus, *Leadership Coaching* (Coach 22, 2005)

# View From the Front Line: Disciples Who Make Disciples

The post-modern culture of celebrity and consumerism has given birth to the idea that 'I' am at the centre of the universe. In the YouTube world of selfies and bloggers, it's possible, though mistaken, to view Jesus' call to discipleship as being all about me and my personal development and fulfilment. The truth is that while God does care personally and intimately about each of his children, Jesus' kingdom is radically counter-cultural in that it is all about multiplication and giving sacrificially to others. We will be known as Jesus' disciples not by the way we post a Facebook status, but by the way we love one another. Written into the DNA of every disciple of Jesus is a mandate to go and make disciples who, in turn, make other disciples. Our mission is to multiply beyond ourselves into the lives of those around us. God is raising disciples who make disciples.

As I look back on my life, it is littered with examples of men and women who helped me grow, because they took the time to multiply in me what they each carried from God. While programmes can help us, we ultimately need to be coached by real people. This is an intentional and relational process that Jesus calls us all to be involved in. What do you carry that you could give away?

At this point in my life, preaching and prophesying are two of the gifts that I regularly use, but I only developed effectiveness in these because others took the time to walk through the multiplication process with me. I learnt through the four stages of watching, sharing, doing and repeating.

As a teenager, freshly filled with the Spirit but needing some mentoring in the art of hearing God's voice clearly, I was hugely helped by an older man called Bob who was a member of our youth leadership team. Spotting some kind of gift in me, Bob would regularly get me alongside him to watch as he prayed and prophesied over others in our youth group. Before long, we began to share this privilege, albeit a little reluctantly on my part. Bob would often approach me during a youth worship time and ask, 'What is God saying to you at the moment, Phil?'

Sometimes I would have a slight impression or idea that God had placed on my heart and I would share this with Bob, often not thinking it was any more than my own imagination. Full of confidence that I had indeed heard from God, Bob would then ask me the follow-up question: 'Who is it for in the room and what do you think you should do with it?' If I didn't know immediately, Bob would give me a few moments before coming back and repeating the question. In this way, I learnt not to settle for general prophetic revelation, but to ask God for specifics that would bless people in a clearer and more definite way. Bob would then help me approach individuals with the prophetic word I was carrying and have me share and pray with them. Our discipleship had moved from purely watching, to sharing and doing. Within just a few years, I was using this very same method to develop others, by repeating the process in their lives.

Likewise, I developed in the gift of preaching through the multiplying effect of others in my life. Growing up in a Baptist church, I listened to my own father preach brilliantly week after week and was also exposed to some very gifted teachers of God's word. Terry Virgo, John Wimber and Michael Eaton were all huge influences on me and I devoured their teaching, whether in person or listening to recordings. But my big step forward was when I was allowed first to share in a teaching time as a 16-year-old. We were working our way through the whole Bible, and I was asked to share a summary of eleven books of the Bible from Ruth to Job in twenty minutes! I'm not sure it was the most riveting talk, or most helpful, but it was a start.

After finishing school I embarked on a gap year, volunteering for an American church in Columbia, Missouri. As the year went on, I was given more and more opportunities not just to share in teaching but to preach in my own right. I vividly remember struggling and straining over what to preach on one such occasion. I had spent a fruitless afternoon in the study books and was looking in vain for some inspiration. With the meeting due to start in a few hours, I began to panic. Sweat beads formed on my brow, icy shivers of adrenaline coursed through my body and I began to plot my escape route. Picking up the phone, I called my team leader to bail me out. 'I can't do it,' I pleaded. 'It's just not coming together and I've been trying for hours. Please can you preach instead?'

My leader paused on the line before asking me one simple, God-inspired question. 'Phil, has God called you to preach or not?'

'Erm . . . yes, he has,' I replied, with some consternation in my voice.

Quick as a flash, his response came back, 'Well, you'd better get on with it then!' as he promptly hung up the phone!

I did preach that night and it was probably the best message I had ever given up to that point in my life. God moved powerfully, but not because I felt powerful. God moved because he always equips those that he calls. The kingdom first expands through obedience, not skill or confidence. I only learnt this lesson well because someone took the time to allow me to do something that required faith and courage. I have repeated this same process with many others through the years because I know how vital it was for me in my own growth as a disciple.

The apostle Paul, as he was teaching on the subject of generosity in finance, gave us a vital principle when it comes to multiplication in the kingdom. He said, 'Now he who supplies seed to the sower and bread for food will also supply and increase your store of seed and will enlarge the harvest of your righteousness' (2 Corinthians 9:10).

God gives us bread and seed. The principle here is that in every provision of God there is something that benefits us and something that benefits others. One is to eat and the other is to sow. Paul is spelling out the only sustainable and satisfying way to live life as a Christian. If I live only to consume, I end up in selfishness and starvation, because I have not used what God has given me for increase. If I live only to give away, I end up in exhaustion and fatigue, because I too need to eat to stay healthy. The answer, says Paul, is to enlarge the harvest of righteousness through God's supply and increase. With every good gift I receive from the Lord I must ask, how can I give this away to others too?

Disciples of Jesus naturally multiply wherever they go. Freely you have received: now freely give.

## Prayer to Start Following Jesus:

*If you openly declare that Jesus is Lord and believe in your heart that God raised him from the dead, you will be saved.* (Romans 10:9 NLT)

If you have read the pages of this book and realised you have not yet made your own decision to become a disciple of Jesus, here is a simple prayer of faith you can follow to start your journey.

Father God, I thank you that you hear my prayer and that I can come, just as I am.

Thank you for sending your son Jesus to die in my place. I recognise that I need you and the forgiveness you alone can give. Thank you that your love is bigger than my mess and your mercy can cover all my sin.

Please wash me clean from every wrong thing I have ever done, said or thought in the past, present or future. I receive my new identity as your child, free from shame and raised with Jesus. I turn my back on living my own way and embrace a new life of following and learning from you.

Fill me now with your Holy Spirit and give me power to live as light in this world. Thank you Father!

*But to all who believed him and accepted him, he gave the right to become children of God.* (John 1:12 NLT)

# Endnotes

1. Dallas Willard, *The Great Omission: Reclaiming Jesus's Essential Teachings on Discipleship* (Monarch, 2006), p. xv.

2. Eric Russ, *Discipleship Defined* (Xulon Press, 2010).

3. Mike Breen, *Building a Discipling Culture: How to release a missional movement of discipling people like Jesus did* (3DM Publishing, 2017), Kindle locations 980–981.

4. George MacLeod, *Only One Way Left* (Wild Goose Publications, 2000), p. 38.

5. Brene Brown, 'The Power of Vulnerability', ted.com/talks/brene_brown_on_vulnerability

6. LeRoy Eims, *The Lost Art of Disciple Making* (Zondervan, 1978), p. 57.

7. See Edward T. Hall, *The Hidden Dimension* (Anchor Books, 1966).

8. Excerpt from speech by Theodore Roosevelt, *Citizenship in a Republic*, 1910, theodore-roosevelt.com/trsorbonnespeech.

9. Sidlow Baxter, reported in Charlie Jones and Bob Kelly, *The Tremendous Power of Prayer* (Washington Square Press, 2009), p. 46.

10. E.G. Carre, *Praying Hyde, Apostle of Prayer: The Life Story of John Hyde* (Bridge-Logos Publishers, 2001), p. 111.

11. Ruth Heflin, *Glory: Experiencing the Atmosphere of Heaven* (McDougal Publishing, 2016).

12. Charles Spurgeon, *Spurgeon on Prayer and Spiritual Warfare* (Whitaker House, 1998).

13. Richard Foster, *Celebration of Discipline: The Path to Spiritual Growth* (Hodder & Stoughton, 2008).

14. William Law, *A Serious Call to a Devout and Holy Life* (Forgotten Books, 2017), pp. 168, 164.

15. Bill Johnson, *Strengthen Yourself in the Lord* (Destiny Image, 2007), p. 68.

16. Philippa Lalley, 'How are Habits Formed: Modelling habit formation in the real world', research article published in *European Journal of Social Psychology* Volume 40, Issue 6 (July 2009), pp. 998–1009.

17. Raniero Cantalamessa, *Life in Christ* (Liturgical Press, 2002).

18. Quoted in Bill Hybels, *The Power of a Whisper* (Zondervan, 2010), pp. 11–12.

19. George Dana Bourdman (Author), Bob Mumford (Compiler), Jack Taylor (Compiler), *The Kingdom: The Emerging Rule of Christ Among Men: The Original Classic* (Destiny Image Publishers, 2008).

# Also Available...

**Naturally Supernatural by Wendy Mann**

The supernatural life that Jesus modelled is not reserved for a few 'superstar' Christians; it is meant to be the normal life for every believer. All Christians are called and equipped by God to see his Kingdom break in as part of their day-to-day life. This book unpacks over ten years of Wendy Mann's journey of learning how to live a naturally supernatural life. It is full of faith-building stories, inspiring insights and practical tools.

**Developing Prophetic Culture by Phil Wilthew**

In *Developing Prophetic Culture*, Phil Wilthew articulates God's heart for creating vibrant churches and Christians who know how to hear God's voice with great clarity. Using more than two decades of experience, Phil unlocks some of the keys to building environments that develop prophets and prophetic people in a healthy, Bible-honouring and Jesus-centred way.

http://store.kingsarms.org/

PGIL2023USA